OMG!
I AM A MOM NOW

BookMedia

OMG! I AM A MOM NOW

All information, techniques, ideas and concepts contained within this publication are of the nature of great comment only and are not in anyway recommended as individual advice. The intent is to offer a variety of information to provide a wider range of choices now and in the future, recognizing that we all have widely diverse circumstances and viewpoints. Should any reader choose to make use of the information contained herein, this is their decision, and the contributors (and their companies), authors and publishers do not assume any responsibilities whatsoever under any condition or circumstances. It is recommended that the reader obtain their own independent advice.

FIRST EDITION: 2020

ISBN: 978-81-948058-2-3

Published by BookMedia
www.bookmedia.co
info@bookmedia.co

OMG!
I AM A MOM NOW

A.N.S.W.E.R.S. TO EVERY BRAND-NEW MOM'S
EMOTIONAL CONCERNS

BookMedia Publishing House
Pondicherry, 605001, India

DEDICATION

To my son:

He had made my life complete by promoting me as a mother and he is the sole reason behind the origin of this book.

To my family:

My family had been my constant support system and I am what I am today because of my family.

Thank you.

PRAISE FOR THE BOOK

You nailed it in your own way. Whatever field you choose, you go with utmost hardwork and research, even on tiny things which reflects in each word of your book. It is a must-read book for all moms to be and new moms which gives them strength in much needed areas and makes the post-partum period a better experience. It is the first book by Abinaya that I have read and I am sure it won't be the last. I'm waiting to read your next book and wishing you all the very best.

– Dr. Balamani, Medical Officer, Thiruvarur.

The author beautifully illustrates the unexpressed difficulties of a new mom and the ways to overcome those difficult times. This is definitely a best guide to all brand-new moms. This book covers the most common issues faced by a new mom and gives the best practical solutions. I would suggest this book for all new moms, to handle the situations in a better way. This book would be the best gift to be presented to new moms. I really had a very bad habit of comparing my child's growth with other children. After going through the A.N.S.W.E.R.S. strategies, I have made up my mind to stop comparing and to just concentrate on what best I can give to my child.

– Mrs. Vidhyalakshmi, Finance Specialist,
State Street HCL Services.

This book by Abinaya is the need of the hour, where young moms are struggling to cope with the multifaceted responsibilities, contrary to our previous generation where most of us opted to be homemakers only. The strategies she outlines are very simple and practical and can be adopted by any mom aspiring to travel through the journey of motherhood joyfully.

– Dr. Haseena, holistic healer and principal,
Dr. AKB'S Mission Hospital and school of Pharmacy

Every mother passes through nostalgic moments and unexpected expressions that are even difficult to share with anyone. I think this book can be a friend to those moms who are passing through this juncture of the life. The A.N.S.W.E.R.S. strategies connect to each and every moment that a first-time mom feels.

– Gunjan Agarwal, Assistant professor,
Department of Commerce, Siliguri.

What I like about Abinaya's book is that, the book starts with Rest and asking if everything is alright with the new mother. Because there could be a lot going on with mothers who are taking care of their baby, be it their first-time experience or even if they have been supportive of other mothers during their journey of raising an infant. My most valuable takeaways from the book are to stop giving parental advice to mothers. As instead of my contribution helping their journey, it may add more stress to them. Rather I would tell them to work on understanding their emotions with Abinaya's 4 Rs technique and to track their progress to a new and better version of themselves, who is confident of being a great mother to their child. I would recommend this book to all newly married couples and new parents, so they can learn, share and prepare themselves for a great parenthood with Dr. Abinaya Vijayakumar. They could also experience a stress-free motherhood, as mastered by the author with her own personal experience.

– Saleem Mohammed, Software Engineer,
BA Continuum Pvt. Ltd.

Journey from being a daughter to motherhood is an adventure and it transforms you into a different person. Mental and physical stresses are part of this change. Abinaya through her book, OMG! I AM A MOM NOW explains to all brand-new mothers how this journey can be simple, fun-filled and at the end gives ultimate satisfaction. I feel this book as a priceless asset. I appreciate Abinaya's effort and wish her all the best.

– Suresh Babu, Principal, Mumbai.

This book is a perfect step-by-step guide to all new moms on preparing themselves to their motherhood and also about parenting your infant. A must-read reference manual to make life easier during pregnancy and post pregnancy, by stepwise guidelines from a super-mom who has gone through the balancing act of being a woman and the multiple roles she plays, plus her major turning point of her life - her motherhood! P.S: A must-have guide book for new dads too!!

– Rajeev Nagavkar, Entrepreneur, The BREW Digital Advertising.

First of all, I would like to congratulate Dr. Abinaya for her efforts to pen down the experiences and lessons despite being a busy mom. You have always been an energetic and enthusiastic person and it's no wonder you are coming up with such a book from your personal experience. This piece of work is going to be a worthy addition to the library of recently married couples. Yes, it gives a 360-degree view on the precious yet complex post-partum weeks. The expert interviews from different specialists are definitely a desirable inclusion. Thanks for giving me an opportunity to share my views and knowledge as a tiny contribution. Keep writing and best wishes to all your endeavors.

– Dr. Rajesh Kannan N, Assistant Professor, Department of Psychiatry, Theni Medical College and Hospital, Theni.

Abinaya V has written a remarkable book about the new mom's stressful motherhood, seeking a helping hand. The book is so elegantly written, so much understanding about new mom's concerns and is going to be a definitely useful book for all new moms. The A.N.S.W.E.R.S. for new moms in this book defines not just a methodology but a way of life for succeeding in life. It is so apparent that it would work. It is a beautiful book that could change all new moms' life.

– Rupakumar Pradhan, CFP., CWM,
Chief Financial Planner & Director, SmartFin
Wealth Management Pvt. Ltd., Bhubaneswar

"THE ONLY SOURCE OF KNOWLEDGE IS EXPERIENCE". First of all, I want to congratulate and thank Dr. Abinaya for sharing her experience with public and create awareness among mothers. This book will be an excellent resource for first time mothers who are stressed, not confident and struggling to be a successful mom. Being a pediatrician, I've seen many mothers who are facing the challenges in their post-partum. I strongly recommend them this book. It will be a treasure and will guide them further.

– Dr. Sudeendar Nanthakumar, Consultant Pediatrician,
Dr. Nantha Kumar Clinic, Vellore.

I wish this book has been released 23 years ago when I delivered my first son. Regardless of brand-new mom, this book has so many values which could change the life of every woman in a better way.

– A.V. Ajitha, Health Visitor, Chennai

Kudos to Abinaya for taking up this most challenging topic of womanhood. I also congratulate you for being a solution provider than playing a victim. I love the way you approach the topic, great sequence of events, eloquently put perspectives and solutions in simple terms. This book is highly recommended for all new moms and new dads out there. It is important that they understand what they are going through and to plan on how to sail through as a team.

– Dr. Joseph Thomas, Chairman-
Santo Group of Institutions, Bangalore.

I strongly believe that this book is a legacy which has to be passed on to every new mom for many generations to come. This book has so many practical values which on implementation will bring a stress-free life.

– Shyamala, Pharmacist, Chennai.

FREE BONUS

FREE BONUS #1: Videos of 5 expert interviews.

Check http://drabinayavijayakumar.com/video-interviews/ for the interviews.

FREE BONUS #2: Get 10% discount on your first online consultation with Dr. Sathiya, Gynecologist using **CODE: OMGMOTHER10**

FREE BONUS #3: Get 10% discount on the first online consultation with the Dr. Sudeendar, Pediatrician using **CODE: OMGBABY10**

FREE BONUS #4: Get 10% discount on the first online consultation with the Dr. Rajesh Kannan, Psychiatrist using **CODE: OMGMIND10**

FREE BONUS #5: Get 20% discount on any one of the nutrition/ fitness programs under Mrs. Kripa Dharmaraj in KD vs. KG using **CODE: OMGFITMOM20**

FREE BONUS #6: Get 10% discount on first online consultation with Mrs. Teena Abishek in Pregnancy Care Center using **CODE: OMGPCCC10**

FREE BONUS #7: Get 20% discount on any one of the pre-pregnancy/pregnancy/lactation classes under Mrs. Teena Abishek in Pregnancy Care Center using **CODE: OMGPCCP20**

CONTENT

INTRODUCTION

Have you ever thought of, how a day would be in your post-partum? Have you ever prepared or thought of preparing yourself, for the days to come after your child is born? Have you ever stood in front of your mirror wondering how you have changed over the recent months of pregnancy and post-partum? Have you ever felt missing the old you? Have you ever worried thinking about whether you would really be a good mom? Have you ever wondered how you are going to lose your baby weight? Have you ever cried aloud for you couldn't do it anymore? When was the last time you had a candle light dinner with your husband? When was the last time you watched your favorite Netflix show uninterrupted? When was the last time you read your favorite book by the side of a window with a super brewed hot coffee by your side? YOU ARE NOT ALONE! There are millions of brand-new moms out there who feel the same way as you do. Research says that post-partum blues hits every alternate mother and post-partum depression affects around 1 in 9 women. It can have an adverse effect on the well-being of both the mother and the child; yet 1 in 5 women keep quiet about their symptoms and therefore remain untreated.

This book is for brand-new moms who are tangled in the cobweb of stressful motherhood seeking for a helping hand to untangle and live stress-free. "OMG! I AM A MOM NOW" is the secret formula for brand-new moms to make them TURN ON the simple switch of confident mindset to lead a more relaxed and happy motherhood. This book clears the mind-blocks of a new mom which complicates the process of parenting and has made it into a simple transparent process. Being mindful is the new age parenting tool. It is powerful and simple at the same time. The A.N.S.W.E.R.S. strategies are going to be a game changer in parenting as well as the savior of your professional and marriage life.

1 year ago, I entered into the phase of fourth trimester with my baby boy in hand thinking that the struggle is over and I finally did it! But little did I know that the real challenge is yet to come. I was very well prepared for my pregnancy and childbirth that I handled it really cool and smart, in the process of which I forgot that I need to prepare the best for my post-partum. As a result, I knew nothing about the fore coming challenges. Months together I was stuck in the process of understanding my child, knowing what to do and what not to do (a never ending process), trying to be the BEST MOTHER, expecting credibility from others, self- doubting my abilities, feeling worthless because of the physical and mental exhaustion. I was body shamed for my overweight. I was humiliated for how I looked. As I was already friable, this broke me even more and shattered me into pieces. Though I had a great cushion from my family who was trying to make me feel confident and happy, there was something wrong deep inside which was never revealed and repaired. I was waiting for some magic to happen that will bring back the HAPPY ME, the AV who was fit, beautiful and confident. I was waiting for someone to make this process easier for me, to come up with a simple solution that will wipe off my tears, least before completing my maternity leave and getting back to my job. Later I realized that only if I take charge of being responsible to change things in my life, things are really going to change.

Throughout this book, I am sharing simple mind strategies that you need to reinforce in you to get into what is called as a stress-free, happy and confident motherhood. This book will bring a change in your ideology on BEST MOTHER, make you confident and relaxed by which I am sure you could handle anything and everything that comes your way. This book will fast track your waiting queue and give you the golden ticket which you were yearning for. I bring in my life experiences in this book so that you can understand and don't repeat the same mistakes which I did. Also understanding that if you want to change things around you in your life, the real change must begin within you- THE INNER SELF.

Ever since I started following this secret formula of simple mind strategies, people around me started noticing a huge difference in me – A Happier, Confident and Relaxed Version. My friends and relatives started asking me that how I could manage to be so relaxed having an infant and how I am completely stress-free when it comes to my professional and personal life even after having a kid. I have been religiously following these mind hacks to maintain a calm, composed mindset in parenting as well as in other aspects of my life. Few of my friends who were brand-new moms as well, started looking up to me as an expert and sought my advice for stress-free parenting. Once they started to implement these formulas in their life, they started getting results and they are leading a stress-free motherhood too. These strategies are not so complicated and difficult to practice, but these are something very fundamental which we forgot to implement, in the process of making things complicated and tangled in order to find a solution to our problems.

I promise you that if my friends and I can come out of all those tough times through these simple strategies, I am sure you can do it too. If you follow these secret formulas, you can unlock your inner self – a happier version of you, which in turn can unlock the treasure of happy motherhood.

At this point, you can pick your option to choose your way to motherhood- the old skeptical mother in you who is tired of waiting for the answers to her problems or the new confident mother who is aware that the answers are within her, who can now take control of her mind and shine with a smile as a happy mother. So, if your choice is option 2, I welcome you to The Brand-New Mom Community and want you to jump into the first chapter right away to get into the real action mode.

CONGRATS MOMMA!!!
A BRAND-NEW MOM

You have done one of the most amazing things in this world-bringing a new life to this world. As a result of which, you may feel tired, exhausted, weak and sore. It is completely normal to be that way. After all we are human beings too, not some superpower.

Childbirth is an amazing process, a victory of physical exhaustion and physiological remodeling, where the body undergoes a series of changes along with the surge of numerous hormones to give birth to the baby. As a result of which your body becomes exhausted in all means. You would feel energetic at a moment, but at the very next moment you would feel like giving up, very tired and down. It is completely normal to feel that way, just after you have given birth to your child. You are so powerful that you have brought a new life into this world. Remember not everyone can do what you have done. You have done a miraculous job that it is time for you to pat yourself on your back. Take a minute to look back on your journey of pregnancy till childbirth to cherish most blissful moments, to feel the real determination in you. Now is the time to treat yourself for your achievement. Your mind and body need to be taken care of, need to be healed and the one miracle medicine which could heal your mind and body over time is REST.

REST ! REST !! REST !!!

You have successfully accomplished a spectacular and commendable act of carrying your baby for 280 days (may be even more or less) and just delivered it safely. Now you have to give your mind, body and soul enough time to recover, rejuvenate, relax and to get back to normal. Some may feel alright very soon! Some may not.

You may now have the urge to put your shoes on all the other activities that have been piling up in your checklist. But all those can wait for a little longer. You need to appreciate yourself, pat yourself for the commitment and success in bringing your little one safely from your womb to the outside world. The best way to appreciate yourself is to give that enough time to heal yourself from within.

Coming to my post-partum experience, I formulated a 20-20-20 rule which worked the best for me. This simple rule could help you as well. Here it goes:

First 20 days (Day 1–Day 20): Complete rest for first 20 days. The life cycle is just simplified to bath-eat-feed-sleep-repeat. Nothing else. This would help you to relax your mind, body and soul. By following this, you give an ample time to your sutures (episiotomy/ Caesarian sutures) to heal completely. Remember to walk for few minutes every few hours in order to maintain the blood circulation in your legs.

Second 20 days (Day 21–Day 40): After 20 days, you can slowly start going for a small home tour everyday but remember- Do not strain much. You still have to rest whenever possible and it is not recommended to go far away from your home.

Third 20 days (Day 41–Day 60): By 40 days, you would feel much more healthy and refreshed than before. Continue taking small walks each day in your terrace or outside your house or in a nearby park. But remember you are still recovering. Give this time to plan for future. Nothing works well without a clear plan in mind.

You can now plan and prepare yourself, mind mapping a rough sketch of how you could go about the things in future, so that you would be much more clear and ready to start by the end of the 60 days.

I strongly recommend a minimum of 60 days rest-frame to give you a complete resting and rejuvenating time which would yield the maximum results.

If you are that person who doesn't have 60 complete days to relax, then I would recommend the following rules of rest for post-partum which are also effective as tried and tested by thousands of women across the globe. They are-

1. **5-5-5 BED RULE** for post-partum recovery from healthymamahacks.net by Karen L. Kostohris
2. **Rule of 2** as mentioned in the book, "YOUR BEST BODY AFTER BABY"

5-5-5 BED RULE:

In the book, she advises post-partum moms *plan for 5 days IN the bed, 5 days ON the bed and 5 days NEAR the bed.*

5 days in the bed – you should be completely in rest except for getting up for meals, restroom and bath.

5 days on the bed – The next 5 days, you can be up and about a bit more, but make sure that the *majority* of your day is still in bed!

5 days near the bed – Now comes the next 5 days, where you can be little more active but still near your bed, meaning you can do little up and about walks with baby, within the house.

Rule of 2:

This basically means 2 weeks around the bed, 2 weeks around the home and 2 weeks around the community. Rule of 2 as per the book:

2 weeks around the bed – You must be resting in the bed most of time, except getting up for food, restroom and a little walk inside the house.

2 weeks around the home – As you are now in third week of post-partum, many of you may feel much better physically, your post-partum bleeding might have reduced. Some may still experience weakness, feel tired and have heavy post-partum bleed, and it is completely normal. If you are feeling recovered to a great extent, you can have a short casual walk in your street, but remember you must be within reach from your residential locality and not too far.

2 weeks around the community - By this time, many post-partum moms feel relieved of the physical exhaustion which was present in the past. You could now take those "breastfeeding breaks" and could probably go around for a pedicure, after all it is been so long since those feet of yours experienced a pampering. You could quickly hang out for a cup of coffee with your best buddy.

This is the minimal time frame of resting I am suggesting about. But remember to be slow in the process. Many women would require longer resting time. You know your body better than anyone else. Listen to what your body tells you and rephrase the resting rules according to your needs to make a personalized REST RULE for your post-partum recovery.

I required months together to recover physically and psychologically and I'm completely fine with it. No two mothers are the same. So, follow what your body needs and give the maximum time because you deserve it.

IS EVERYTHING ALRIGHT?

> **When I had my first child, I was too embarrassed to tell a single soul that I wasn't the over-the-moon, picture perfect new mother I was supposed to be.**
>
> **– Stephanie Ruhle**

Are you feeling weird inside?

Do you feel like crying?

Do you feel irritable or feel lack of attention from others at home?

Do you feel like harming yourself or your baby?

If answer to any or all of these questions is yes, then it might be a signal that you are suffering from post-partum blues or depression. Post-partum blues is just a normal physiological process which happens due to sudden drop of hormones in your body during your post-partum. It will fade away in a week or two. If post-partum blues get worsened, it may lead to post-partum depression.

Many a times, women don't speak out their problems, considering it as their fate or destiny to go through such tough times.

So, keep a track on your symptoms to see if it is progressing or regressing, to have a check on your psychological wellbeing. Express to your family members about how to feel inside every now and then. Take help of your support system in order to come out of your problems.

MASTER YOUR MIND

"EVERYTHING IN LIFE STARTS WITH YOUR MINDSET FIRST AND ACTIONS SECOND. YOUR ACTIONS FOLLOW YOUR THOUGHTS, YOUR BELIEFS AND IDEAS. TO MAKE A SHIFT, TO FREE YOUR ENERGY: START WITH GETTING YOUR MIND RIGHT, AND THEN TAKE ACTION."

– Sylvester Mcnutt III

What would be the end result of giving those A.N.S.W.E.R.S. to your questions in mind, without you having any clarity in your mind?

Do you think you could go ahead and implement those strategies when you are not even in the right mindset?

How does it make sense when I show you the path to happiness when you are still blindfolded?

Do you think you can go ahead in the right path to reach your happy destination without clearing your mind-blocks?

And that's where mastering your own mind plays can an inevitable role such that you are ready to unlearn few things from the past and to learn new things in the present for a constructive future. Without any further delay, let us look in to the core values of our mind to realign and rewire itself to taste the confidence, success, happiness and love in your life. I have formulated the 4'R's technique which could help you to effectively master your mind.

They are:

- Remove your self-doubt

- Reassure yourself

- Rebuild your confidence

- Record your life

REMOVE YOUR SELF-DOUBT:

> **"SOMETIMES IT IS NOT THE LACK OF ABILITY BUT THE LACK OF CONFIDENCE THAT PREVENTS US FROM ACHIEVING WHAT WE REALLY WANT. SOMETIMES, IT'S DOABLE, BUT SELF-DOUBT MAKES IT IMPOSSIBLE."**
>
> **- unknown**

Self-doubting is the unpleasant surprise planned by the motherhood to brand-new moms. Self-doubting your parental capabilities can actually be heartbreaking and not-so-expected good news to you. Whenever you doubt yourself, you are taking the wrong turn to get lost on your way to happy motherhood. Here is my **5-STEP-SELF-DOUBT PROOF STRATEGY**:

1. **Stop right there:**

   Whenever you realize that you have self-doubting thoughts popping up in your brain, put a big red traffic light to stop it right there. This is going to help you in prevention of further worsening the brand-new mom's potential and thinking capacity.

2. **Talk to someone:**

   Whenever you have self-conflicting thoughts, open up about the same to your close ones. You might actually become aware that you are not alone in this self-doubting brand-new moms club and also get some help using their self-learnt answers.

3. **Learn to be with right people:**

   "You are the average of 5 people you spend most time with."

   So, choosing the right people around you is always very important in order to remain positive in your life. You could get a partner for this process, a person who is also trying their best to leave self-doubts and stay positive. Hold each other accountable in order to get the maximum benefit.

   As Darren Hardy writes in The Compound Effect:

   "According to research by social psychologist Dr. David McClelland of Harvard, the people you habitually associate with, determine as much as 95 percent of your success or failure in life."

So, stay healthy, active, relaxed and focused to whatever that comes your way. Find out your negatives that are holding you back and work towards it each and every day. Learn that skill, develop the required attitude and sharpen your entire learning curve. Even if you face any failure, try to be kind and constructive on what has to be changed in order to avoid failure in future rather than being so hard on yourself.

4. **Course-correct:**

   Don't wait for a perfect plan to start. You can always course-correct during the process. Start with a rough plan and proceed towards your goal with an optimistic behavior.

5. **Celebrate your tiniest success:**

   Now that you have started investing in your personal development to remove your self-doubt, I want to share this pro-tip with you, Try to celebrate even your tiniest success. It may be anything very simple like setting a "ME TIME" for yourself and that you have done it successfully on Day 1. Or it may be losing one kg in your weight scale. Don't forget to treat yourself for your commitment in doing that task. Get yourself your favorite ice cream, a new dress, a makeup accessory or whatever you like for that matter.

You need to believe in yourself in order to see success in whatever you take up. Once you learn to remove your self-doubt using the 5-Step-Self-Doubt-Proof-Strategy, you will now have to reassure yourself that everything is going to be fine.

REASSURE YOURSELF:

Once you have removed the stone of self-doubt away from your eyes, it gives you a much clearer vision in life. You need to reassure yourself that everything hereafter is going to be absolutely fine and you are never going to turn your back to your problems. Instead you are going to face them with a positive mindset and warrior skillset. Stop asking others for validation. Learn to reassure yourself. Expecting reassurance to always come from others puts you in a weaker situation thereby sending self-doubts to your brain and shatters your self-confidence. If you are someone who is constantly asking the same questions over and over again to people around you, you start feeling low with your self-confidence and also others start seeing you as a nagging weaker soul as you keep asking the same set of questions over and over again. How can you reassure yourself? Start writing down in a journal about all your positive reviews, your appreciated works and your strengths. This will help you to reassure yourself immediately when you look into the journal, thereby cutting down further self-doubts, instantly boosting your self-confidence and leaving your mind clear, happy and focused.

REBUILD YOUR CONFIDENCE:

> **"NO ONE CAN MAKE YOU FEEL INFERIOR WITHOUT YOUR CONCERN"**
>
> **–Bernard M. Baruch**

Building confidence is the strongest foundation for your inner peace, personal and career development. Confidence is born only when you try something out of your comfort zone. So dare to take that bold step in your life if you want to live a happy and well-balanced motherhood. Positivity and confidence are like twins. The more positive you are, the more chances of getting confident and looking confident. Don't carry your negative thoughts on your back from past, as it would be really heavy on your way to happiness and contented lifestyle.

If you ever thought that you need to be perfect in order to be confident, you are taking the wrong train. Perfection is the worst enemy of confidence. If you seek the perfect way to do things, whatever efforts you put in, you are not going to feel confident. Never try attempting to be a perfect mother in order to please someone else. You will never be a confident mom if you always try to be the perfect mom which others expect you to be. You are already perfect to your baby. On the other hand, perfection is a relative term. What seems perfect to you, may seem to have flaws in other person's point of view. So don't go by perfection, just start being satisfied by every honest effort that you have put in. Whenever someone gives you 10 reasons of procrastination that you can't do something, show them 100 reasons why you are a capable person to do it. Don't forget to expose the END POINT - "The Winning Moment" to everyone.

The only person whom you can trust and be confident about you in all times of your life, is you. If you have failed to trust yourself, then no one else is going to help you out. It is moreover like shutting off your eyes and complaining that the world is dark. Learn to open your eyes in order to see the beauty of the world. Say it aloud that you are the best mom your child can ever have. Try to learn from your mistakes and mold yourself to be better than yesterday. Once you try to build up the confidence to be a better person, you will definitely feel your ability to face any challenge and find out answers to any number of questions that pop out in your life. There are two ways to rebuild your confidence:

-Mirror-Me Talk

-Affirmations

MIRROR-ME TALK (MMT):

This "The Mirror-Me Talk" is the term coined by me in order to build my confidence, to witness my weakness and strength in the mirror every single day without fail. Everyday I spend the first 10 minutes looking into the mirror and giving myself a big fat smile and an energetic "GOOOOOD MORNINGGGGG". This way I feel the positive vibration of my energy to the maximum and I assure that I am Positive for that beautiful Day. That one person in the mirror gives me that instant transparent feedback of how I am, how my day is going to be. On the other hand, whenever I feel not-so-good in the morning, I exactly see and hear, how I look and sound. I make sure that I stand in front of the mirror and have a positive self-talk until the mirror-me feels energetic and is ready to rock the day. It is merely like the *"show instead of tell"* concept where you show yourself how beautiful you are when you look confident rather than just telling yourself for hours together. Remember that "you are the most beautiful, only when you are the most confident".

ACTION POINTS:

- Go in front of the mirror for first 10 minutes once you wake up in the morning.
- Greet yourself with that beautiful big smile and most energetic "Good Morning"
- Say how positive you feel about the day. Prepare yourself.

If you are not so positive about the day, say it aloud about what *your* challenges *are.* Don't stop there. Just go ahead and list out what are the solutions you have for those challenges. Check for the practical possibilities of implementation of the same. Or if you don't have any solutions, check out who can help you find those. Prepare yourself to approach the challenge with a positive mindset. This optimistic self-talk in mirror will make you feel recharged and will help you face the day with so much confidence. Take this first 10 minutes of the day to prepare yourself for the day – "for the positive day".

AFFIRMATIONS:

Affirmations form a major aspect in building self-confidence. Affirmations impact your subconscious mind over time and bring about a great impact in your progress and development. New moms tend to forget the power of practicing affirmations as they are bound to new responsibilities and having to do chores 30 hours in a day. But I don't want you to do that grave mistake. Write down positive affirmations in a piece of paper or journal to boost your confidence. Every day, make it a point to spend few minutes during your mirror – me talk to say aloud the affirmations that you have written in order to bring about the positivity and progress in your life. Here are some of my favorite affirmations, feel free to add one or more points from here to your list of affirmations if you really like it.

NEW MOM AFFIRMATIONS:

- I am the best mother to my child. I know better than anyone else what my children need.
- I am doing an amazing job. Not everyone can do what I do.
- I will always trust and follow my maternal intuitions.
- I will take good care of myself in order to be a happy, confident and content mother and I truly deserve it.
- I become a more confident mother with each new day.
- I am creating positive and lifelong memories with my children.
- Being a mother has made me look and feel more beautiful.
- I am an outstanding role model for my children.
- I am allowed to ask for help as a mother.
- I do not expect to be a perfect mother.

- I am doing my best as a mom and that is enough.
- Motherhood reveals my strengths to me.
- Asking for help does not mean I'm a failure.

Few sites to download mom affirmations for free:

www.bertmanderson.com/100-positive-affirmations-mom/

www.motivationping.com/mom-affirmations/

www.personalcreations.com/blog/positive-affirmations-for-moms

www.pickanytwo.net/affirmations-for-moms/

ACTION POINTS:

- Write down a list of positive affirmations that you could relate to your life. You can insert few affirmations from the lists available for free in the above websites.
- Feel free to include one or more affirmations from my favorites if you really like them.
- Spend few minutes every single day to say these affirmations aloud or in front of the mirror (as a part of mirror-me talk).
- Maintain a journal to write down your emotions on Day 1 and keep writing it every day as how you feel when you recite those affirmations. As a part of 30-DayMind-block Knockout Challenge, write it till Day 30. Now check on the progress by looking at Day 1 and Day 30 of your journal. I am sure there would be a great difference. That's the real power of affirmations.

RECORD YOUR LIFE:

"If your life is worth living,

It's worth recording"

– Tony Robbins

Most of successful persons follow the habit of journaling. This is what Hal mentions as Scribing in his book, 'The Miracle Morning'. The power of journaling is beyond expectations. It is a productive habit which one has to inculcate in his daily routine in order to achieve personal development in every aspect of his life - be it physical, mental, spiritual, relationship, work, career, wealth etc. Many top leaders like Barack Obama, Sir Richard Branson and Aristotle Onassis follow the habit of journaling every single day. When this simple strategy of journaling had worked for millions of people out there, why do you want to reinvent the wheel? If you have never done journaling before, I insist that today is the right day and now is the right time to start practicing the habit of journaling in your life. Everyday spend few minutes either in the morning, evening or night to write down your challenges, your goals and your gratitude. Many people feel stuck at some point of time in life, but journaling can really bring out the hidden reason behind the stuck-feeling when you actually put it down in words. This way you will now understand what your blocks are and how they are holding you from marching ahead in the path to live a desired life. Make it a habit to write every single day atleast few lines. Write down your goals and steps of actions to be taken towards achieving your goal. This will keep you on track to reach your goal. If you are tangled in new responsibilities of being a mom, write down what your difficulties are. Take some time to think of what steps can be taken in order to come up with a solution for the same. Check into the A.N.S.W.E.R.S. section to see which can be your problem-solving secret formula. Use the formula consistently in order to fetch the result of happy and relaxed motherhood. Many life coaching sessions, parenting training, relationship boot camps insist the importance of maintaining a journal in which you write down your gratitude, affirmations, difficulties and habits to change in your life, steps taken towards it and your own vision board or action board depicting how you want to be in future. Journaling is a proven method to assess your strengths, weakness & goals thereby stimulating your brain and signaling it to work towards remodeling and bringing about a great positive change in life. Start recording your life by journaling every single day starting from today.

I think by now, you would have flushed out your negative thoughts, self-doubts, start journaling and confident to fetch your answers from within you in order to bring about the change in your life.

GET A.N.S.W.E.R.S. TO YOUR EMOTIONAL CONCERNS

As you are now power packed with a positive mindset, building a confident soul by removing your self-doubts, reassuring yourself and ready to fetch your answers to implement in life to live a happy and relaxed post-partum as well as confident motherhood. A in A.N.S.W.E.R.S. stands for 'Ask out for help.'

ASK OUT FOR HELP:

> **I've learned a lot since I was a new mother. My approach to struggle and shame now is to talk to yourself like you'd talk to someone you love and reach out to tell your story.**
>
> **– Brene Brown**

This is the first and foremost strategy to deal with your mental health downscale. Ask out for help! Say out loud that you don't feel good! That things aren't ok! Talk out with your family how you feel. Even the Holy Bible says," Ask and it will be given unto you".

Asking out for help doesn't mean that you are weak. You are actually very strong to come out of your way to ask out for help from others. You are no less than a mother if you ask out for help. No one is going to steal the "MOMMY TITLE" and the crown from you. You are the one and only mother your child has. Stop believing in the concept of super-mom, where the mother does all the work by herself. It's mere stupidity! C'mon, when you have a support system at the distance of your hands, grab it! If you don't have, build it. Explain to your family how you are feeling about this whole new process, the need for the support system and how it works. Have you seen an elephant playing in sand, where the elephant takes a whole lot of sand and puts on its own head making itself dirty and filthy? Not asking for help is exactly the same where you complicate things and keep worrying that things are complicated.

When you cannot advocate your feelings yourself, how do you expect someone else in the world to understand you on their own and help you voluntarily?

Don't you think it is not logical?

So, learn to advocate your thoughts and feeling. Don't shy away from asking out for help. Trust me. It will change your lives in a better way in the journey of motherhood.

For instance, consider these situations, you go to a doctor, you say what your problem is and the doctor examines you and prescribes medicine for the same. You go to drug store and ask for a medicine by its name and the chemist knows what meds to give you. You go to a grocery store and askout for a vegetable that you need, so that the shopkeeper can help you to find that. The same rule applies everywhere. Even here too!!!

If you think the whole system has to change, to bring the change in society which in turn brings the change in you, I'm Sorry, but you are boarding the wrong train that will take you nowhere. The change what you expect should begin within you. You will impact to bring about a change in the way that society sees, which inturn will bring about a drastic change in the existing system in the society.

Tell your dear ones if you feel something unusual inside. Many-a-times you may hesitate to speak out due to the fear of JUDGEMENT of you as a bad mother by people around you. You tend to fear that people may say "NO" when you ask out for help. But this isn't true. 9 out of 10 people agree to help when asked for. So why can't you take a chance? It is not the people around you who are not helping your situation, but your inner fear that actually worsens the situation.

Now, I will tell why you have to speak out your problems and ask out for help, so that you can understand the need of the hour to speak out. Most of the times, **silence is considered as approval**. If you are silent, it means you give your fullest consent to the situation prevailing there. People around you will think that you are comfortable doing the things that way.

Next reason is **you need to clarify** on certain things if you aren't clear about what and how to do. Supposing you have a latching issue with your little one, if you don't talk out and think it is normal to be that way, you are committing a blunder which will impact your health as well as your baby's health. If on the other hand, you have a random conversation with your friend, who is also a mother of a child, say, six months older than your child, she may come up with a solution for your problem when she could actually relate to her initial days of breastfeeding. The solution can be really simple like using a breast shield or syringing to pull out the inverted nipple. And that's the happy ending for your problem. It is mandatory that you speak out to solve the problem.

The third reason why you should talk to others is **to reassure that you are not alone in this problem**. Many had faced it or are facing it every single day. Maybe they are waiting for rescue as well. So, stand for yourself and speak out for you and everyone else who are like you. You may not know that you are setting up an example or a change in the society.

Fourth important reason is talking can actually **ease out your stress and pain** that is dumped in your brain. Sometimes, you don't actually need a solution but listening ears. You would feel a great relief after pouring out all that is bothering you inside. You get refreshed and become more relaxed.

Fifth reason is that by **not speaking out** the problem, you are **not just ignoring the problem but worsening** it even more. For example, imagine yourself as the volcano which is prepping itself with bouts of smoke being pushed out, getting ready to burst open. If people living around the volcano considered it normal and didn't take action for moving to safe places, they are being dumb. The damage is going to be worse as time passes. When the volcano bursts, there may not be any golden egg of "TIME" in people's hands to save their lives and valuables. Similarly, if something is not right within you, you need to open up it up right at the beginning. If not, it may eventually turn into post-partum depression and psychosis, which is a serious threat to the both of you and your baby's health. Speaking at the right time is as important as asking out for help. So do it at right time- the very beginning of the problem.

Sixth reason is that if everyone considers not to speak out, then this will remain as **the attitude or lifestyle of the fore-coming generations** as well. The mental health problem of the new mother will remain on the darker side of the room for ages to come. This will be "The New Normal" and people will start living with it and there is not going to be any improvement in the society.

So break the chain, start speaking out your problems and ask out for help. If you don't do it today, you will regret it for a life time.

Here I would like to mention about a real life incident which was told to me by my psychology mentor when we had a telephonic discussion regarding this book. This is the story of a 28 years old female, who had come to psychological counseling to my mentor. She was a mother of 8 months old boy baby, who was brought with history of agitation, shouting and one episode of throwing the baby away. When she was enquired in detail, she disclosed the following history:

Her child was exclusively breastfed till then, didn't sleep properly at nights, woke up from sleep very often and took breastfeed. It took around 4.30 AM for the baby to go into deep sleep. She hardly slept for an hour each night. Her husband worked in a company, went for 7 AM shift, so she used to wake up again at 5.30 AM to cook breakfast for her husband. Then she continued to do the day to day household chores, took care of baby's needs once he woke up. In the afternoon, she washed clothes and made snacks/milk ready for the small shop ran by her family. She had been busy all day and didn't have proper sleep at nights which had made her restless and agitated. Due to cluster feeding, the woman had developed sore nipples which was giving her immense pain. This was more like oil added to burning fire, intensifying her restlessness. She hadn't disclosed how she had felt and even others had failed to notice the difference. The built-up anger, restlessness and immense pain caused due to sore nipples had rooted deep down causing depression.

This in turn had affected the woman's bonding with her child. She started accusing the child for all that troubles she is into. She started feeling that everything was in place before the child's birth and it had tossed the other way after the child birth. During a quarrel with husband, things started taking a rage and she ended up shouting and throwing the baby away from her as she felt the baby as the sole reason behind all her tough times.

When the mother-in-law was called in during the counseling session, she had told that she was not aware of all those problems that her daughter-in-law was going through till the very moment of counseling because her daughter-in-law had never expressed anything of that kind. Every morning she went up to her daughter-in-law to help in cooking, but she had refused it saying that she would manage it all by herself. She was really clueless.

When her husband was told about how the wife feels, he was totally astonished to see the behind story. He said he had no idea of all that his wife had gone through. He felt that it would have been so simple to tackle if she had opened up a conversation about the same to him. He added that he would have got lunch from the company canteen, if she would have told that she couldn't make it up in the morning to prepare his breakfast. After speaking with everyone in the family, the psychologist had advised the woman to speak out her problems with her close ones and to ask for help. Also, as the baby was 8 months old, the mother was advised to start complimentary food to the child. After a month, when the women came back for follow-up, she was feeling much better as the family was aware about her problems and so they were readily available to help her. The child started sleeping for longer hours at night so the mother was also able to sleep longer. Ideally, the sole problem was she did not speak out her problems, ask out for help, but in turn was waiting for someone to understand it by themselves. If she would have opened up earlier, she wouldn't have gone through so much of tough times. Life would have been much easier and her bonding with the little one would have immensely increased. So, I would highly insist you to speak about your problems to your near and dear ones. Ask for help if you are not able to do it alone. Use your support system for the benefit of you and your child.

ACTION POINTS:

- Ask out for help. Never withhold yourself from speaking out your problems and stepping forward to ask for help from others.
- Remember. The change must first begin within you.

RECOMMENDED BOOKS TO READ:

Non-Verbal Communication by Marshall B. Rosenberg

The next letter "N" in A.N.S.W.E.R.S. stands for No to parental advice.

NO to parental advice:

People around you will always bombard you with,

"When I was a mother back then...."

"What I did to my kids was that..."

"Why it happens because..."

"How I used to deal with this situation back then was..."kind of stories and suggestions without even listening to what you actually want about it.

It is very common that if there are 10 people around you, they will give you 10 different opinion for the same problem out of which hardly one may turn out to be right. The worst case scenario, neither of all is right. The irony is, these kind of suggestions puts the new mom in edge of the knife making her to get afraid and doubt herself on her capabilities as a mother, bringing her to the age-old doubt of new mom which is "Will I be a GOOD MOTHER?".

So the simple easiest way to refrain yourself from these unwanted self-doubting situations is to stop listening to everyone around you. In other words, a big "NO" to parental advice. You can actually accept any of those suggestions if they come up with a scientific base or proof that it actually works. Otherwise stay wise and stay away from unwanted parental advice.

Because advice on parenting and baby's wellness are taking turns every once in a while. Hence people are not up-to-date which can lead to 'many not so true baby advice which may pose a threat to baby's health. The new mom who is subjected to the ball game of hormone variations, just wanted to hear that she is doing a great job instead of bombarding with unwanted advice.

If you feel someone entering into your personal space which you are not comfortable with, that is the clue that you should stop listening to them. Turn on your mind to "FLIGHT MODE" so that there is no way their words entering into your brain and heart to cause damage to your internal self and external life. The black board theory will explain in detail why you have to stop listening to all parental advises.

THE BLACKBOARD THEORY:

The brand-new mom is like the brand-new black board which is empty. You must choose carefully on what you want to write in that board of motherhood. If something is written wrong, you can still wipe it off but the traces will still remain and will never be the same new shining black board. Listening to all parenting advice that comes your way, is like letting everyone to meaninglessly scribble in your blackboard which will eventually lead you to a shabby pointless board depicting a skeptical, anxious and something-is-always-missing kind of motherhood. On the other hand, analyzing every parenting advice and taking up only those of which have scientific base and proven results, is like cautiously choosing which person to take the chalk and write in your blackboard or in other words, choosing whom you want to dictate so that you can effortlessly write yourself on that board. Be wise in choosing the writer/writings on your black board. If you are already ahead of this phase where someone already scribbled on your board, it is time that you are awake and aware of it. The sooner you hold the chalk, the lesser the damage and higher the chances of cautiously rewriting in your blackboard.

The third letter "S" in A.N.S.W.E.R.S. stands for **"Stop"**. Stop doing these things if you already doing them.

A) Stop Complicating Things:

Keeping it simple always works. You need to believe it first that your baby is doing absolutely fine and healthy. New moms are so skeptical when it comes to their baby's health. I've seen a new mom who wanted the doctors to do a COVID-19 test for her baby just because the kid had bouts of sneezing once. I understand the mom's concern on her baby but it's the unnecessary fear that I wanted to address, that is building in her mind which is going to make things no better but bitter. If your baby has a mild running nose, it could be a mild respiratory illness and not necessarily be Pneumonia. Just keep in mind about the Warning Signs or RED

FLAG signs which your doctor told you to look for. Otherwise staying cool and keeping it really basic and simple as much as possible always works pretty well.

If you couldn't clean up the entire house, you need not to necessarily do so. Maybe you could do it a little later or can reschedule the cleaning time for the next day. Just relax momma! It is not a criminal offense if you don't clean the entire house that particular day. If you couldn't take care of baby alone, then don't do it alone. It is neither good for you nor for the baby. Stop stressing over things and making it complicated.

THE VICIOUS CYCLE OF COMPLICATION:

Complicating is a process of further complicating your already complicated problems. Does it sound complicated? Haha! let me explain further. Complicating things is like a vicious cycle:

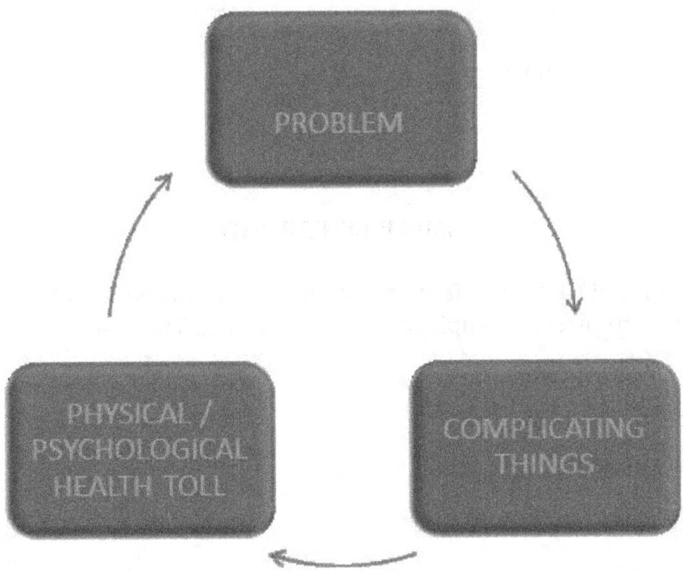

THE VICIOUS CYCLE OF COMPLICATION

Always try to be calm and focused before assessing and handling any situation, not just motherhood but anything and everything that comes your way. This will make your ideas clear to process your thoughts faster and to find your solution even sooner than before. Every baby is not the same. Every day of the same baby is not the same. Every mother is not the same. Every pregnancy of the same mother is not the same. Understand this reality before stepping on to your next day in motherhood. When you understand what you can't expect, you won't be disappointed if it doesn't happen. This breaks the vicious cycle in the level 2- complicating things—which then leads to a SIMPLE LINEAR PATH.

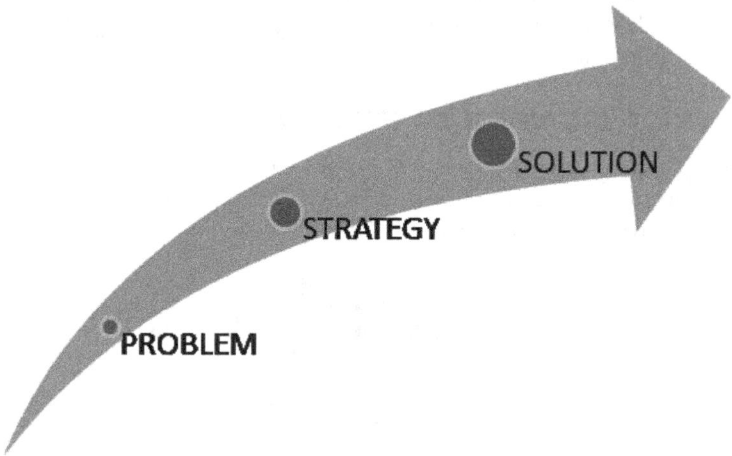

SIMPLE LINEAR PATH

I wanted to discuss few scenarios and aspects which the brand-new mom usually complicates way too much. They are,

1. Messy home
2. TMI syndrome
3. Being the world's best mom
4. Fear of bad mom title

MESSY HOME:

One important problem of every brand-new mom is to keep the house clean. Messy home can be a real time challenge for first time mothers. It is one aspect where the new mom complicates way too much.

What if a moderate to massive earthquake hit a home resulting in shattered things, spilled over food on the table, clothes thrown all over the house, making it a dirty home? This is the scenario of a new mom house many-a-times. I am not exaggerating. It happens and it is completely okay to be like that.

If you ever come across any new mom house which is neat, clean, shining walls and face-reflecting-clean floor, it means that the lord of timing had favored her just this one time. Few moments later, this cannot be the scenario what you would be looking at. Now you are that new mom. Don't give a shit to have a clean home all the time. It's okay if it's not. By this, I don't mean that you can have a dirty home all the time, what I want to convey is that don't stress out if you put your extra effort only to find a messy home again in a day or two. If you are someone like me who don't know when and where to start with, here are my tips:

1. **ONE AT A TIME:**

   If you think of cleaning the entire house in a single day, May your soul rest in peace. ☺ haha. Stop stressing too much and being too hard on yourself. Try to show some mercy on yourself. So, take one portion of the house in a day for cleaning.

2. **PRO TIP:**

   The more exposed area of the house has to be your top priority. So if that big hall, your bedroom and restroom are the most visited area by your guests, clean that area first and keep it shiny. No one is ever going to peep into that unused drawing room or the empty small bed room every time of their visit. So, it is okay to clean it once in a while, or clean it on a later date.

3. **TAKE HELP:**

   Do not do it all by yourself. Take help from others which includes- your partner, mother, siblings, in-laws or friends. By this way, you could ease out the stress of putting all burden over your shoulders and it could be even more fun and exciting thing to do.

4. **HIRE A MAID:**

   If you are economically stable, I highly suggest that you hire a maid at a nominal charge. It is similar to that of getting two mangoes by hitting with a single stone.

   I will tell you what those two benefits are in a single hire-

   - You don't have to stress yourself on a clean house, so that you could be relaxed about the visitors' arrival.
   - You could actually spend more quality time with your little one rather than cleaning your dirty house.

5. **TRY MINIMALISM:**

   This is my favorite. Sell that old lying sofas that occupy most of your space in the hall, pass on your old dresses that doesn't fit you anymore to your siblings or donate it to a charity home or sell it on e-bay. So ultimately it is less-things-less mess-less stress kind of living. Try it and you will remember me in your prayers thanking me every day.

RECOMMENDED BOOKS TO READ:

10 Minute declutter by S.J. Scott

Simply cleanby by Becky Rapinchuk

ACTION POINTS:

- Look into these tips to deal with a messy home and see what would be helpful to you.
- Start implementing on the same immediately.

TMI SYNDROME:

TMI syndrome stands for TOO MUCH INFORMATION SYNDROME. Knowingly or unknowingly every brand-new mom has TMI syndrome at one phase or the other.

One thing which goes without saying is "Google is the brand-new mom's best friend". New moms tend to google every silliest doubt, every symptom to find the cause, every possible side effect of the little one's medications and every possible reason for the change in color, consistency and frequency of poop of the little one. I myself have done it countless number of times too. But, my dear friend, just remember, too much of anything is good for nothing, leading to a disease which I call as "Too Much Information Syndrome" (TMIS).

It can actually turn the table, making the scenario worse than it was before. Internet is the treasure of information and knowledge. I do agree, but you need to understand the basic dynamics of any search engine. It doesn't process your exact scenario to find answers, instead just the keyword that you enter for searching. Google lists you all the relevant files with the mentioned keyword. But you need to understand "one size doesn't fit all". TMIS poses a threat to new mom's already existing anxiety, from making the worse to the worst. For instance, if you type abdominal pain as the keyword in search, you may find the disease listing going from simple gastritis to stomach cancer. Not necessarily everyone who have abdominal pain end up having stomach cancer.

Simple 2D principle to avoid TMIS:

6. Digital detox
7. Draw a line

Digital Detox (DD):

This is my first and foremost suggestion. Digital detox is nothing but refraining yourself from all the gadgets/social platforms/search engines. I know I sound too old like your granny who will tell you to stop using that phone all the time which was the one and only thing we grew up listening to. But trust me, it works like magic. It is basically shutting of your doors to all those unwanted anxiety, comparisons, widely available ready information with no filters, commercial branding etc. It is too tough to DD in the beginning, but you will thank me for this later.

Draw a line (DL):

I know this would be your preferred option than the former one. But the real challenge comes with drawing the line, where you are exposed to all the threat putting you into more anxiety, but you need to draw a line as where to stop and what to take with you. Many times, new moms start looking at picture perfect moms and start feeling bad about their life that doesn't look anything of that sort. It is more like, going to the best ice-cream shop in the town, looking at all tempted flavors but you would be holding one scoop of very old vanilla flavor ice-cream. So, you have to do the reality check, take only positive feedbacks and refrain yourself from negativity. You must analyze the information in the internet, seek its scientific base and evidence of research and then if that information passes through all these channels of filters with strong hold, you can go ahead and take those values from it.

It is entirely up to you to choose DD or DL to escape yourself from getting trapped into TMI Syndrome.

BEING THE WORLD'S BEST MOM:

When someone mentions "The world's best mom" phrase, I really pity them. There is no such thing that actually ever exist. You can never be the world's best mom and it is no way necessary for you to be. All that you actually need is to be your child's best mom which you already are. So stop stressing out for something which in context is not true first of all. You don't need any judge to say that you are a best mom. Every mom in this world is a best mom.

FEAR OF BAD MOM TITLE:

If someone bullies you or comments on your way of parenting and say that you are a bad mom, you don't have to really give a shit about it. Just pity them as they are trying to express their inability and not yours. Who are they to judge you in the first place? So why do you want to care about it? You have nurtured your child in womb for 9 full months without sharing any sort of burden or grief and you are continuing to give the best for your child each and every single day. No one ever knows what it is to be in your shoes. So **STOP LISTENING TO ALL THOSE BULLSHIT!!!** You are absolutely wonderful.

b) STOP BLAMING YOURSELF:

Are you the mom who blames herself if the child has a mosquito bite?

Are you the mom who blames herself if the child isn't sleeping well?

Are you the mom who blames herself for the baby's weight when she sees the other baby in road being chubbier than her baby?

C'mon. Don't be so hard on yourself !!! If your child is meant to be bitten by that mosquito that day, you cannot do much help. There may be any of those many reasons why your child isn't sleeping well that day. It may be too hot, may be too cold or whatever. There may be many reasons for your child to look different from the other child of which one main reason is that every child is unique. So, stop blaming yourself for every single thing that doesn't go well.

Playing that self-blame game is always destructive. Taking responsibility of whatever good or bad happens in your life is actually a healthy habit by which if something goes wrong, you can analyzes your past to look deeper what went wrong. This is way more different from accusing yourself for anything and everything that went wrong in your life. The self-blame can actually be the reflection of your past failures, negative experiences and childhood trauma. But your past has got nothing to do with your present and future. Remember you always owe the superpower of rewriting everything only if you realize *where you are* and decide on *where you want to be (my favorite phrases from the book- The Miracle Morning)* and take control of your life from now on.

Every brand-new mom is so anxious about this new phase of responsibilities which she hadn't handled earlier. Hence the mother tends to put herself in the cage of blame if something or the other goes wrong with the child. As long as the child is fine, the new mom would never do it. But once a small negative change happens in her child's life, she takes up the entire blame, thinks that it is her negligence which had caused the problem in her child.

I had done the same mistake of blaming myself in my early post-partum when my son was admitted in the intensive care unit due to chikungunya. I started blaming myself for all those pain and sufferings he went through during those days of hospitalization. I completely believed that it was my sheer negligence which had caused this huge toll on my son's health. Though my family remained very supportive to me, my relatives started accusing me indirectly for my negligence in parenting leading to what my son was suffering then. I accepted every bit of accusation as I myself strongly blamed me for all that was happening to my son. This broke me into pieces when it came to my mental health. I was feeling weak, sore and shameful for not being a good mother, which was my sole responsibility back then. Beginning from there, I started accusing myself for every small negative thing that happened to my son. As days passed, I started losing my confidence in every aspect of my life. One fine day, I realized that I had no future if things go this way. Instead of blaming myself, I started taking responsibility for everything that happened in my past and decided to march ahead in my motherhood without blaming myself for anything in future. Once I consciously made this decision, I implemented the same in every aspect of my life since then. Life is so easy once I stopped blaming myself.

Blaming yourself is actually going to make you feel down and depressed which is going to make things worse and not in anyway better. Blaming yourself is a way of weakness which you exhibit to the world with or without your knowledge, thereby giving your consent for someone else to blame you or in other words, 'tag you' in every problem you and your child are facing currently and going to face in the future. So never give the key of your weakness to others as they can steal your home of happiness one day or the other.

ACTION POINTS:

- Stop blaming yourself.
- Take responsibility for everything that happened in your past, make a decision to march ahead without self-blame and to start trusting your abilities.

c) STOP COMPARING WITH OTHERS:

Do you compare yourself with other new mothers?

Do you compare your child's growth, weight, developmental milestone with other children?

If the answer to the above questions is yes, then you have to stop doing it right now.

The grave mistake of every brand-new mom is comparing themselves with others. Comparing yourself or your child with others for validating yourself is not a healthy process. I will tell you why –

- Makes you feel inferior when you are not on par with someone you compare with. This in turn will break your confidence and your bonding with your loved ones.
- Makes you feel superior when you are doing a great job when compared to someone else. This will impact your brain asking for more validation by comparing with others every single time. This is not healthy too.
- Comparing with others is never a fair process. Every mother is unique and every child is unique. You can never compare a fish and a bird as both are two different creatures and have their own unique abilities. Similarly comparing yourself with another mother in the process of parenting or comparing your child's weight with another child is mere stupidity and foolishness.

How to stop comparing with others:

Whenever you become aware of comparing yourself with others, stop right there. Do not encourage the process. If you see another woman in post-partum who had lost her baby weight faster than you, instead of comparing and feeling low, you can go to her, open up a healthy conversation to get pointers on how she had lost weight. You can try to implement those tips in your life to see if it brings out change in you as well.

Similarly, if you see another mother who is bottle feeding her child and you are breastfeeding yours, instead of feeling superior, go towards her, open up a healthy conversation, ask about her pain points and check whether you could help her in some way.

This change must begin from you, which on the long term can make you a better person than what you are today. Holistic practicing of not comparing yourself with others as well as not comparing your baby with other baby can make you stress-free to a larger extent and can help you lead a happy and confident motherhood.

CELEBRITY MOM SYNDROME:

Most of the new moms tend to compare themselves with the celebrities who have also given birth to child at the same time period. They would compare their post-partum weight loss and fitness journey, their child's weight gain or general well-being with that of the celebrity mom. This is what I call as "CELEBRITY MOM SYNDROME". This syndrome leads the new mother to a state of self-conflict, worthlessness and debilitate their maternal abilities. For me, it was an Hollywood actress who had delivered her son just a week earlier than me. It all started when I randomly came across one of her photos in a social media, starring herself and her son. I was taken aback by her fitness where she was the same old actress, the way she looked even before her pregnancy. The second thing that took a strike in my mind was that cute chubby kid. I could guess the age of the baby at a glance, all the mothers out there can agree with me. We do this right? Immediately, I went on google hunt to view more of her family pictures, her delivery date and even the vacation with the little one. Now my life started running faster as a flash news inside my head. Here I am with the same weight as I was in my 39th week of pregnancy, not even losing few grams - even more plumpier, with my abdomen looking like as it is rolled with thick quilt, unable to spot my curves and with a huge hanging tummy. Anyone and everyone who doesn't know me, would be readily asking me which month of pregnancy I was in and connection between me and the outside world was barely two trips to a nearby coffee shop and for vaccination of my little one. I started feeling down, depressed and devastated. It took me many days to gather up my courage to defend my negative thoughts in order to bring about a change towards living a happy and confident life.

I am sure many of you would have done it too. If you are doing it, just stop it right there before it takes a deeper depression root in your minds. You are going to gain nothing but disappointment on comparing yourselves with the celebrity moms. Just don't be hard on yourself. You deserve certain respect for having done this great job of bringing a life into the world and taking care of all their untold needs every single day. Just breathe through. This is not your entire life. This is just a part of your life and I am sure it is going to be the most memorable part. To make or break, it is in your hands.

PICTURE PERFECT MOM:

Have you ever come across that perfect mom moment in someone's insta page and freezed for a moment saying, "I am going to be like her." or "Gosh, How can she do this right, when I couldn't? "... Here is the secret to all you mamas, "PICTURE PERFECT MOM" doesn't really exist. They are just virtually created amongst the messy home, about to-give up mom and naughty kid. If you personally know any mom with that perfect click on their social page, take a minute and ask them politely how they got it done. They will reveal you the entire back story bringing that big sigh of relief in your face that they too face the same challenges like you. And say it to yourself that the cleanest home, groomed mom and smiling cute baby is a timely freeze of once in a month or a week time moment. So stop over-thinking and stressing out yourself in order to keep it that way all the time, which is not going to happen anyway.

Stop comparing your life with others and learn to start enjoying your life. I am sure life will change in a much better and happier way than you have ever expected it to be.

WORK WISELY

The letter "W" in A.N.S.W.E.R.S. stands for Work wisely. In other words, "WORK SMART, NOT JUST HARD". As a new mom you are bound with numerous works starting from taking care of baby's needs, household chores, cooking, taking care of the needs of your husband and other family members. At this juncture, I would like to give you a "PRO TIP". Don't try to do every single work by yourself. Try to divide the work among the family members. Do important chores which could be done only by you, but otherwise if there is any work which can be done by others please feel free to have them do that chore. For example, in babysitting, there are certain things which can be done only by you like breastfeeding the baby. So you can do that. But there are other things in babysitting which need not be necessarily done by you like bathing the baby, changing of diaper etc. In such cases, you can share your work with your family members to do that, instead of, just you taking care of everything. A smart boss doesn't do every work himself He assigns the job to the right person and get it done in the right time. So my dear brand-new moms, why be an employee when you can be a boss? Try to be a smart boss.

SHARE RESPONSIBILITIES &SWITCH ROLES:

You need not do everything everytime. When you have your family members at home, make the best use of the resources you have. If you have completed breastfeeding your child, you can ask help of your husband or others to take care of the child for a while so that you can rest. Though, few people don't come up on their own to help, they'll agree when ask for.

Speak with your family members especially your husband if you could share responsibilities. Explain how important and crucial it is to share responsibilities for the wellbeing of you and your baby. You will get some "ME TIME" (the importance of ME TIME will be discussed in a while under last strategy of A.N.S.W.E.R.S.), some time to relax and rest. You will replenish your body and mind for taking better care of the baby. Also, the baby tends to bond better with the father and other family members as well. Sharing responsibilities can be really life-saving at times to brand-new moms like you. These small breaks can actually avoid putting yourself in the situation of depression and anxiety.

The act of sharing responsibilities can be put into action whenever you feel tired, especially at nights. Sleepless nights are one of the main attributing factors to fatigue, low mood and anxiety. Take turns. Do not stay awake all nights. It can be really exhausting which can affect your health as well. If you stay awake one night to take care of your baby, it can be your husband's turn to take care of the baby the other night. You can pump out the milk in advance and store it so that he can feed the baby as well. In this way, it can be balanced and less exhausting.

Switching roles can actually bring about more responsibilities and accountability in the family. It is a great tool of building the stronger bond at the foundation level.

What would happen if you don't share your responsibilities? You are throwing away your parachute when you are actually jumping off a cliff, which would be of your life saver. You are going to regret it later for a lifetime for having committed a grave mistake of your life. You are going to endlessly search the key to a happier life while you have voluntarily thrown it away into the sea. Trying to fix things after broken is more expensive and time consuming than actually preventing it from getting broken.

Now that you are aware of the benefits of sharing responsibilities and working together, you would wonder "how to do it exactly?" I heard you. Let me guide you through the process. The power of communication is much stronger than anything in this world. It is mandatory that you sit with your family and make them understand about how you feel, what can be done and how to share responsibilities. Don't forget to follow up on the same. Never ever forget to appreciate their effort in sharing your chores. Appreciation is your card for life time access to continue to work wisely by sharing responsibilities.

What if they don't agree to share responsibilities?

Is this question ringing in your head as you read through the above lines?

Let me ask you this question - How do you know that they won't agree without you even asking out? The fear of rejection and judgement by others is what holds every new mother from finding a solution for her problems. You need not be afraid in asking out. You are doing a great job by asking out to help you by sharing responsibilities which could be a one stop solution for problems like depression, frustration and bonding with your family after child birth.

As the child is important to them as well, this act of sharing responsibilities and switching roles can nurture their bonding with child. It is much better than ending up in a psychologist counseling where you end up saying people around you never understood or helped you which was the root cause for your low mood and agitation.

I had a friend of mine who was a brand-new mom too. She had to do all household chores at day amidst of managing the baby by herself. She had to stay awake till late night and also had a disturbed sleep pattern due to frequent feeding of baby at night. Her husband was very busy with his business that he was less aware of all that is happening to his wife, which was gradually having a toll on her physical and mental health. As days passed by, she came to a breaking point of saturation where she actually realized that it was not going to work anymore that way. She came up to me explaining her situation and asking me on what can be done. When I told her that it was high time, she should open up a conversation with her husband. She agreed to do the same. They sat down and discussed on the same which was an eye-opening moment to her husband who never realized it until then. Since then, her husband started to actively take part in sharing responsibilities with her. He even took turns every alternate night to take care of baby while my friend had pumped the milk into bottle and slept peacefully those nights.

Sharing responsibilities doesn't just make things easier for my friend to take care of baby but also initiated a new chapter of more love, care and support instilled in their relationship as well.

WELL BALANCED WORK -PERSONAL LIFE:

Are you worrying about your fore-coming days of going to back to work, leaving the child at the home? Does that separation anxiety of future troubling your present?

I have you covered as well....

WORKING MOM GUILT: What are you guilty of? Is it about supporting your family? Is it because you have to give a secured future for your kid? Or is it for melting yourself to give that shining desired lifestyle to your kid? YOU DONT HAVE TO BE.

You are doing an amazing job of perfectly balancing the game of juggling with your balls of work, family and kid. Take this moment to pat yourself on your back because you are tremendous and you deserve it. Not everyone can do that.

If at any point of time, you are looking into a stay-at-home mom and feel envious, just remember her on the other hand, wish to be a working mother just like you. Both of you are doing great, sticking on to your priorities and giving your fullest effort in your parenting.

How to have the perfect work-life balance?

Schedule your priorities:

Work while you work, play while you play. So, be that working women when you work and be the mom when you are at home. Never take the office work carrying to your house and never take the mommy guilty strapped with your shoulder while leaving for work.

Give your fullest in your role:

If you are back to home after your scheduled work (9–5 or whatever shifts you are in), don't go back to it even mentally before

9 AM next morning. All those pending jobs are still going to wait for you the next morning, so worrying don't lift few files off your table.

Otherwise, you should be productive at the first place, finishing your works on time. Fix your deadlines and stick it on to your desk. Abide by it and strike off all that is in the To-Do list for that day before leaving to home in the evening.

Never get carried away in thoughts regarding your office tenders, reports and reviews at times which is meant to be with your family and especially your little one. Giving your 100% in the limited time is solely what your child is expecting from you and I know you can do justice for that expectation.

RECOMMENDED BOOKS TO READ:

1. The fifth trimester
2. Job escape plan
3. 4 -Hour work week

The first book will practically guide you on steps of what to do and how to handle work-life balance when you return back to your job.

The second book tells you on how to quit your not-so-your-type job, before building up your successful entrepreneurship online being at the comfort of your home, enjoying the freedom and quality time with your loved ones.

The third book will exactly take you on the path of investing yourself in the right job with as minimal as 4 hours working per week, thus making it possible for you chuck that mom-guilt and to enjoy the maximum time with your family.

EFFECTIVE FINANCIAL PLANNING

The letter "E" in A.N.S.W.E.R.S. stands for effective financial planning. Whenever it comes to adding a new member to the family, it puts a tight string around the neck when it comes to budgeting. Experts say that the expense in the family increases by 10% in the first three years of the child and additional 10% increase after three years of age due to educational expense.

An effective budgeting can actually lower your stress and keeps you well prepared for the baby's expenses. The ideal effective planning begins from Day 1 of your marriage or at least from day 1 of planning for a child. This way, you have a huge amount of time to get things in place leading to a stress-free financial independence when the child arrives. Let me frame it in two time frames of financial planning –

Before delivery and After delivery.

Before Delivery:

- Check for insurance cover on childbirth, either in your office, your insurance policy or under any government policies.
- Learn to live with single income for few months even before you stop working nearing your delivery. This way you will not experience a major setback of suddenly adjusting to single income. It can also build a financial cushion for unexpected expenditure.
- Plan your hospital charges for regular antenatal visits with doctors, scans, blood tests and your delivery expenditure well in advance to keep the money readily available so that you don't have to stress out much during the process.
- Always plan to have an emergency fund of a decent amount of money handy.

After Delivery:

- Minimize your expenditure – cut down on unnecessary lavish expenses.
- Maximize your savings – start Savings Account/Recurring Deposits/PPFs.
- Write down your short and long-term goals, save money accordingly. For example, your baby's first birthday party can be a short-term goal and child's educational expenditure can be a long-term goal.
- Cut down on getting all baby products. You may not need everything.

ARE YOU ON A SHOE-STRING BUDGET ?

If you are on a shoe-string budget or if you are someone like me who doesn't like to spend too lavishly on baby products and items, then these masterstrokes are your take away bonus:

- *Make a list of "Essential" Vs "Non-essential but fancy" baby items.* Baby creams, daily wear clothes, soap, shampoo and baby bed are all essential items. Non-essential but fancy items include baby car seat, expensive baby stroller and costly but rarely used kind of hi-fi clothes (baby may overgrow the size in few months and cannot be used again). Essentials must be bought but you must never go crazy by deals/offers on unwanted non-essentials and end up buying things which you are going to rarely use/never use at all.
- *Plan your delivery at an optimum cost.* Nowadays, it had become way more commercial where the hospitals offer the so-called-delivery packages which includes the room equivalent to anywhere between three star to five star hotel rooms. Remember childbirth is a normal physiological process and all you need is an efficient medical care by your side for safe delivery and not a high-end commercial care. I delivered in a hospital attached with a medical school because of which the charges were very nominal and we were equally satisfied with the care. Many thanks to my Obstetrician who was also a financially-wise person so she insisted us not on spending much of our savings on hospital stay. You could use this saved money out of cutting down hospital expenditure on savings like starting a deposit/PPF on baby's name.
- *Go for pre-loved baby items.* These includes dresses, toys, baby beds, cribs and strollers which were pre-used by elder children in the family or even by the previous generation. It's not only an economically wise decision but also the warmth and positive vibes in the pre-loved goods are magical. In my house, there is a sturdy wooden cradle which is in use for three generations, beginning from my father-in-law and his siblings, then passed on to my husband and his brother, which is now used for putting my son to sleep peacefully. So, find out pre-loved items in your house and if they are in good condition, start using them from now on for your child.

- *If hiring a maid takes a toll on your finance at that moment, it's highly recommended that you take the help of your family-* parents, in-laws- siblings or friends. Ask them to come over or you can relocate yourselves for time being. This way you are also sure that your baby is in trusted hands and so you can also relax for a while without actually worrying about your baby.

ACTION POINTS:

- Effective financial planning is a very important strategy that has to be implemented at an earlier phase in order to lead a stress-free post-partum.
- So if you haven't taken any financial decision so far, it is high time that you discuss with your partner to decide according to your requirements, short and long-term goals.

RELATIONSHIP RENEWAL

The letter "R" IN A.N.S.W.E.R.S. strategies stands for Relationship Renewal. Spending quality time with your dear one can be a stress buster. You needn't go for a great trip thousand miles away. Just a simple house party or a brunch with friends can do great magic. Talk to your husband, share your thoughts and admire him when he looks so freaking handsome in your favorite white shirt. Say him that you love him so much. Talk out your memories down the lane which can put a big smile in both of your faces. Tell him how much the little one had taken after him. He'll be on cloud nine for the entire day. Men will really understand your feelings and support you if you try to make them understand. It is okay if you are having zero libido, but never forget to talk and discuss about it with your partner. This should not prevent you from saying "I Love You" many times a day. An airtight hug, few caring kisses with extra dose of love and cute cuddles will definitely keep up the spark in your relationship and will make your intimacy grow bigger and stronger.

I've heard few of my friends crying that their marriage life had become a big question mark after their childbirth, the reason listed may be anything ranging from "No to Sex" to "Showing her frustration on her husband". But following the simple strategies which I have mentioned above and by taking the relationship renewal agreement mutually, they had a life changing happy transformation. By religiously incorporating the terms and conditions of relationship renewal agreement in your life, I'm sure that it will definitely bring about a great change. Jump into signing the relationship renewal agreement which I am sharing with all of you, don't forget to understand that you are accepting the terms and conditions of the agreement mutually and start enjoying the new version of your relationship which is guaranteed for an extensive tenure of lifetime.

RELATIONSHIP RENEWAL AGREEMENT:

- Don't forget to give your partner that extra special airtight hug every single day. The power of hug is far beyond your imagination.
- Do you really miss him at time? So, what are you waiting for? Grab your phone and call/text him saying "I MISS YOU" "CAN'T WAIT TO SEE YOU AGAIN".
- Everyone loves surprises. Don't forget to hide a little note in one of his daily accessories (wallet/note/car keychain/lunch box) stating how special he is to you, how much you love him or it may even be a best moment from the past of your love life (My personal favorite one).
- COFFEE-MATE: Make it a habit to have that morning or evening coffee together every single day.
- Share your meal time. Make sure that you both eat together at least once in a day.
- Consider yourself as partners. You both are in this together.
- Always compliment him for what a super parent he had been to the kid (I bet. Men love it !)
- Make sure that there is never a day in your lives that you two go to bed without talking to each other.
- Share your household chores so that you have no reason to get angry on him. (I got you! Isn't it annoying if he doesn't help you with the dishes/laundry/cooking at times?).
- Cuddling is like fevicol. It can fix anything and everything.

☺ Don't forget your cuddle time whenever you find some moment of privacy with your partner. (They like it that way, keeping the romance alive).

- Be honest with your partner. Share how you feel. Be raw and realistic with your partner.
- Hang out for a dinner date once in a while. You both deserve it! Take the help of friends/family members or hire a maid, let them take care of the baby for sometime, so that you can take care of yourselves.
- Try to initiate and never always wait for it to start from your partner. (Be it saying I LOVE YOU to cuddling to surprise love notes to talking the problems.) (Men actually have starting trouble at times. So it's okay if you have to start!).
- Be lovers for a lifetime. Irrespective of commitment like marriage, responsibility like parents, try to keep that love alive till the very end of your lives.

ACTION POINTS:

- Go through the relationship renewal agreement mutually and make it a point that both of you stick to do some or all of the terms in the agreement. I suggest that you follow all the terms in order to reap the maximum benefit from your relationship.
- Even if your partner forgets to implement, you have to stick on the agreement and show him the benefits so that he tends to put his maximum effort too.
- Be consistent in your efforts to keep your relationship alive and sparkling. For some, it may work out soon. But for some, it may take more time. You have to patiently wait for the results.

The final "S" in A.N.S.W.E.R.S. stands for **"Start".** Start doing these things if you haven't done before-

a) Start shredding at your own pace.

b) Start stepping up your happy hormones.

c) Start trusting your maternal instincts.

d) Start spending some "ME TIME" –Self-love.

A) START SHREDDING AT YOUR OWN PACE:

As you are just back home after your childbirth, you now start wondering at those hanging belly fat, unpleasant love handles, fat thighs and the whole big new you. Just remember, nature has its own time phrase to make wonders. Your uterus had learnt and expanded to accommodate a 3 kg human inside over the period of 9 months. It had expanded nearly 100 times of its original size to undergo this transformation. So eventually, coming back to size zero is never going to be an overnight magic. Stop stressing yourself much about this. Be proud to be the new you, as you have done something majestic which not everyone can do.

First give yourself enough time to recover physically and mentally. Start with mild cardio like slow walking, beginning with 10 minutes per day. Gradually increase your time and speed of walking within your comfort zone. Never ever compare your clock with others. If some other brand-new mom had lost weight drastically, do not feel low. Just feel happy for her. Open a healthy conversation with her to know what worked well for her. Implement those techniques and see if it works for you as well. You have to be really positive and consistent. Mind plays a major role in fitness, only then comes the body. Cut down those junkie cravings, have a healthy diet. Diet accounts to 80–90% of weight loss whereas exercise accounts to only 10–20% of it.

Nothing is as challenging as child birth. If you can do that successfully, you can do this too.

Physical exercise:

Are you the one who is allergic to this word," physical exercise"?

Are you the one who always thinks that physical exercise is something that is not your type?

Are you the one who always wonder about a hi-fi sexy fit woman in a gym outfit sweating like one of a hell, on that treadmill machine in a sophisticated gym?

If you are that one person who fits into any or all of these above questions, then I have another 20-20-20 rule which is going to be a game changer in your life to turn you into a physically active person. All I need you to do is just walk-walk-walk. No need of costly gym clothing. No need of expensive gyms. Just a casual loose pyjamas and some space in your home is all that you need to achieve your desired weight.

20-20-20 Rule (one more time):

The one common mistake that many new moms do is they want a magic result instantly. It doesn't work that way. Do not try to burn out the maximum by the first day, because if you do that, that's going to be the end of your interest in physical activity. Physical exercise is also a mere form of meditation where you need to go slowly and progress steadily to reach maximum benefits. Remember, "Slow and steady wins the race".

Start with a minimum of 20 minutes of slow walking what I call as snail walk every single day.

Increase it by few more minutes every single day for next two weeks so that by the end of two weeks, you could be able to walk for 20 more minutes i.e., 40 minutes totally. You can also slowly step up your pace of walking from slow to medium in the first two weeks.

From the third week, you could further expand your duration by few more minutes every single day. Do not forget to increase the duration steadily over days. Never jump up the limits in just a day or two. Consistency is the key in the physical exercise when you want to get the maximum benefit. Also, now is the time you could gradually increase your medium pace of walking to intensive pace over the next two weeks.

By the end of four weeks, you could be able to walk for 60 minutes in a day at an intense pace. Getting 60 minutes of physical exercise is more than enough to reach your desired results, if you commit yourself to be consistent with the same pace and duration. When it comes to physical exercise, choose to be consistent over enthusiastic, permanent over temporary. Enthusiastic people would turn up for few days, maximum of 1 week. By that time, they would lose their enthusiasm and feel that it is boring to do and so they lose their enthusiasm along the way. If you ever think physical exercise as a temporary solution, you are going to be busy collecting stones over diamond. Physical exercise has to be a life style in order to bring about a long-term effect on your physical and mental health.

It is statistically proven by many surveys that getting some fresh air each day decrease the stress and purify your thoughts making you feel at ease and rise with confidence back on your own. So, at once you are recovered physically, put on the sneakers that are missing you for a while and get into the street to get some fresh oxygen to your mind and soul. If there is no one to take care of the child, you can even take the child in the stroller along with you. Your child can also have a great sensory stimulation when exposed to outside environment. Also, by this way, it can actually help you to have a better bonding with your little one as well.

NO TIME FOR PHYSICAL EXERCISE?:

If you are someone who always feels that you don't have enough time to do a long stretch of walk or exercise, I have got you covered too. You don't need longer duration to start practicing physical exercise. Do you have a 10 minutes break in between your chores? That's more than enough. I am not kidding.

It may be merely impossible to get longer duration at the beginning of your routine, especially if you are the only one taking care of your newborn. Try to break your schedules into multiple lapses. Whenever you find 10 minutes in between, try to do physical exercise during the time. By this way, you can take 2–6 breaks (20 minutes to 60 minutes) in a day each lasting for 10 minutes to carry out your physical exercise. Doesn't it seem much more possible and easier now? Yes, it is. Where there is a will, there is a way. So stop finding excuses and start finding breaks. If possible, include meditation and yoga in your exercise schedule as their benefits are extraordinary and proven for ages. Be conscious during meditation. Stop thinking about other things while you meditate. Keep your mind and soul at ease and relaxed throughout the meditation. A minimum of 10 minutes is good to start your meditation and yoga each day. Increase the duration during the course.

INFINITY WALK:

If you ask me to list out one game changer in walking to solve your physical, mental and health issues, I would spontaneously utter this phrase "THE INFINITY WALK". This is also known as "EIGHT WALK" in vernacular language. It is the way of walking in the shape of eight or infinity.

"WINNERS DON'T DO DIFFERENT THINGS.

THEY DO THE SAME THINGS IN A DIFFERENT WAY"

This quote is exactly true when it comes to infinity walk over normal walk. The origin of infinite walk dates back to ancient days, where Tamil Siddars existed. They have practiced it immensely. The limelight of infinity walk was when the clinical psychologist Deborah Sunbeck listed out benefits of walking in infinity shape.

It all started when a click of moment flashed in my mind of the videos/blogs I have once read mentioning the benefits of walking in the shape of eight. One prime benefit, which was my need of the hour, is weight loss. To be honest, I never expected a great result following the infinity walk. All that I had in my mind was,

"However, I am going to walk, why can't I try doing that in the shape of eight?"

I started walking in the shape of eight every single day. To my surprise I lost 10 kgs within two and a half months which was ridiculously awesome. People around me started noticing the drastic weight loss in me and was surprised to know that the simple magic behind which was just"The Eight Walk". Slowly, my mom, few of my friends and relatives had started following the same technique and it was yielding them good progressive results too. Of course, everyone may not lose 10 kgs of weight as every human body is unique and different from one another. But what I can guarantee is if you are consistent, I am sure you would see positive results too. I suggest "infinity walk" for every post-partum woman if they wanted to follow one specific physical exercise to lose their baby weight.

As I mentioned it earlier, benefits of the infinity walk are not just restricted to weight loss but it has a huge impact on mental health and many chronic health issues which I would list out soon. For me, the real happiness was when I found two other major outcomes along with weight-loss my thyroid levels were back to normal and my worst aching post viral arthritis (joint pain) was relieved to a great extent.

HOW TO DO INFINITY WALK?:

Ideally, it is said to draw two lines of 6 feet each at distance of 10–12 feet. The figure of 8 must be in north-south direction. But if you don't have that much big space, it's completely fine to use the available space in your living room, terrace or parking lot in your house to do the infinity walk. You can either draw two circles with gap in between or a figure of 8 or place two chairs with an optimum walking space in between and can walk with an imaginary eight in your mind.

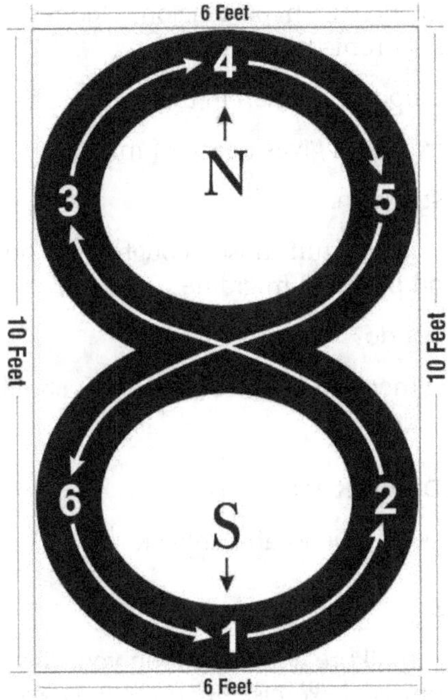

Illustration to show how to do an infinity walk by placing two chairs

8 BENEFITS OF INFINITY WALKING:

1. Promotes weight loss.
2. Relieves joint pain, body pain and arthritis.
3. Regulates thyroid hormone levels in blood.
4. Controls diabetes, hypertension, kidney problems and many other chronic health problems.
5. Improves blood circulation in the body.
6. Relieves stress and gives peace of mind.
7. Cures constipation.
8. Gradually clears stuff nose, cough and headache due to sinusitis and prevents migraine.

Who should not do?

Pregnant women and cancer patients should not practice infinity walk.

RECOMMENDED BOOK TO READ:

1. Infinity walk - by Deborah Sunbeck

ACTION POINTS:

- Try to take small breaks in between your day to start yourself with mild physical exercise. Increase the pace and duration of walking as days go on.
- Take 10 minutes every day for meditation and yoga. Be conscious during meditation. Stop thinking about other things while you meditate. Keep your mind and soul at ease and relaxed throughout meditation.

b) Start stepping up your happy hormones:

The happy hormones are Endorphins, Serotonin, Oxytocin and Dopamine. They are also known as 'feel good' hormones. These hormones are released in your body when you are happy which in turn reduces your stress and makes you cheerful. So this means, do something which makes you feel exotic and happy.

Endorphins are produced when you do things that produces immense pleasure and sense of reward in you. It may be your favorite book which you have read till half way and waiting for you in the shelf near your window. So why wait? Grab it along with a cup of coffee and start over again. It may be cooking your favorite food. It may be watching Netflix/your favorite comedy show. It may be gardening. It may be decluttering your wardrobe. It may be dancing your way out for that pop music. It may even be a conversation after ages with your good old friend. In a nut shell "DO WHAT MAKES YOU HAPPY"

Oxytocin is primarily released during breast feeding which in turn also helps in bonding with your little one. Exclusively breastfeeding your child in turn can de-stress you by releasing oxytocin in your body.

Serotonin and dopamine are neurotransmitters in brain which are primarily secreted during learning process. So try to learn new things every single day in order to stimulate your serotonin and dopamine.

ACTION POINTS:

- Spend some time to do your favorite things in order to release your endorphins.
- Try to learn new things whenever possible during the day. It will stimulate your serotonin and dopamine levels thereby making you happy and stress-free. Also learning will make you a better person than yesterday.
- Try to exclusive breastfeed your baby for the first six months

c) Start trusting your Maternal Intuitions:

When your child is cultivated in your womb, the mommy's instincts are cultivated too. The one common mistake that everyone of us, the brand-new mom does is you start listening to everybody except you. You put your intuitions to sleep. It is that instinct in you regarding your baby whenever you have something to decide on your child. The best part is most of the time the mother's instinct turns out to be right.

I would like to cite this reference from Today.com about an article on Maternal intuitions in which Dr. Victor Shamas, a psychologist at the University of Arizona, firmly believes in the power of intuition. **"I describe intuition as knowing something without knowing how** you know."

Several years ago, Shamas conducted a study of over 100 pregnant women during their first trimester to find out how many could correctly identify the gender of their baby based on instinct. Of those studied, 70 percent predicted the gender of their unborn child correctly, which they described as knowing through a "gut feeling" or a dream.

It is a guiding mechanism installed in every mother to nurture and protect her child. So my humble request to you is to turn on your intuition switch right now. Always listen to what your instinct says and try to follow it. Only you can decide what is best for your child and your instincts will guide you to do it right.

ACTION POINTS:

Listen to your maternal instincts and follow it everytime before you take decision regarding your baby.

d) Start spending some "ME TIME" (Self-love):

> **The very damaging, frightening part of post-partum is the lack of perspective and the lack of priority and understanding what is really important.**
>
> **– Brooke Shields**

Spending some "ME" time can actually rejuvenate you from deep inside your mind, makes you feel fresh, allowing you to relax and start enjoying your motherhood.

The most commonly heard phrase for a new mom that every parenting book, pediatrician, friends and family say is "SLEEP WHILE YOUR BABY SLEEPS". It is actually very true to fully rest yourself and to compensate for those sleepless nights. But once if you have recovered from your childbirth, you can allot this time of the day for the moments of self-love, where you could spend some time to yourself and taking care of what you need. You can even get a hair spa or manicure or facial when your baby sleeps, after all you deserve it!

This "ME" time kindles the self-love in you which would flush out all those frustrations and feeling of worthlessness away from you. You will start feeling new again. If you are a business person, may be now is the time to plot your future growth in career.

Self-love is not selfishness. Getting some "ME TIME" actually make you more relaxed, replenished and refreshed. The mantra to SELF TIME is "DON'T TAKE TIME BUT MAKE TIME." If you try to take time amidst your ticking clock of household work, cooking and babysitting, you cannot do it. Even if you do it once, you cannot hold the consistency. I accept that you being the mother is your biggest priority at present. But that doesn't mean you shouldn't have time for yourself. You have your own dreams, career and goals much earlier. You are a wife before you are a mother. Stepping into the role of mother had greatly shut the door to your other roles for a while. Now is the time you bang open the doors and the magic key to all that is "ME TIME". I hope you are familiar with the proverb "All work and no play make jack a dull child" which exactly fits your shoe for the current situation.

Also, you need to understand the other two aspects of ME-TIME. One is, there will be days in future when your child is grown that they no more need you all the time by their side. One fine day, they will start going to nursery and suddenly you can't accept this transformation in your child. It may lead you to serious mental health problems like depression, anxiety, etc. You need to prepare yourself to be away from your little one every now and then.

Second aspect is, being there for your child all the time irrespective of their needs, can make them so much self-centered and selfish in their growth phase. So take that break and teach them that you need to pamper yourself as you do to them. Make them understand that you have other priorities which are actually as important as them. That's the effective parenting lesson that you enact to your child rather than explaining. Enacting is way more powerful than explanation. Kids always learn from us by 'doing' rather than 'saying'.

Also, use the smart tool of "ME-TIME" called THE POWER OF CHOICE. Don't jump into the process of cleaning the home when your kid spares you with "Me-Time" and convincing yourself that you are actually enjoying it. All those can wait and it will be the same when you come back. Choose what makes you feel happier, relaxing and more of yourself. Choose between loading and unloading. You can say "NO" to extra work (loading your burden) at office while you can nod a big "YES" to brunch with your close friend (unloading your stress). Choose to be more consistent – every day or every week or every month. The power of "Me-Time" is that mere happiness of the "ME-TIME" next day can actually gear up your mood for the present day.

ACTION POINTS:

- After reading this book, sit down, take some time to plan your "ME-TIME".
- Decide "HOW MUCH TIME" you are going to take during "ME-TIME" and decide "HOW OFTEN" you are going to take your "ME-TIME".
- Stick to your commitment on taking your "ME-TIME".
- Be consistent in taking your "ME-TIME" as planned. Never cheat on yourself to skip your "ME-TIME" for other works.

30 DAY MIND-BLOCK KNOCKOUT CHALLENGE

If you are highly motivated to take charge of your life in order to remove your self-doubts, negative thoughts, to build your self-confidence, to validate yourself, bring in a positive change in your life to live a happy motherhood and to unleash 2.0 version of yourself, I highly recommend you to take up the 30 Day Mind-Block Knock Out Challenge. It takes a minimum of 30 days to change any bad habit and to cultivate any new habit. So promise yourself that in these 30 days, you would abolish your bad habits of self-doubting, negative thinking and replace it with new habits of self-confidence, positive thinking and rewiring your mind with A.N.S.W.E.R.S. strategies for a better life.

I will help you through this process of what exactly has to be done in these 30 days:

- Identify every situation where you have mind-blocks in your motherhood and in your life. Write it down in a piece of paper or journal.
- Look into the A.N.S.W.E.R.S. strategies and check which can help to fix you and your present situation. Write it down next to your mind-blocks.
- Now read it aloud. Try to implement those strategies by mastering your mind, whenever you become aware of your mind-blocks.
- It would be difficult for first few times to do it, but remember consistency is the key. Keep working on it again and again till you master it.
- Record your life in your journal every single day starting from Day 1 - your problems, solutions, affirmations towards the solution and the final result you have achieved. Writing

down in your journal makes you more accountable that you will soon develop a habit where there would not be a single day where you haven't read your affirmations and written your journal once in a day. This forms as your core habit and solving your problems by mastering your mind and finding A.N.S.W.E.R.S. within yourself makes your entire life very easy and stress-free.

WHAT DO EXPERTS WANT TO TELL YOU?

Now that I have insisted you enough about the importance of mastering your mind and implementing the strategies to tune your mind in order to bring about the change, let us look at what experts want to tell you. I am happy that I had the privilege of interviewing five experts in various fields. I have interviewed a Gynecologist, a Pediatrician, a Psychiatrist, a Fitness Coach and a Lactation Consultant.

INTERVIEW WITH THE GYNECOLOGIST

Contact Dr. Sathiya (Gynecologist) through mail to: s.sathiya.dr@gmail.com

Don't forget to use the CODE: OMGMOTHER10 to claim 10% discount on first online consultation with Dr. Sathiya.

ME: **What are common pain points of a first-time mother, when she comes for a post-partum visit to a gynecologist?**

Dr. Sathiya: Common pain points are,

- Pain in the episiotomy suture site and low back ache in case of vaginal delivery.
- Pain over the C-section suture site in case of C-section.
- Breast engorgement.
- Heavy bleeding per vagina.
- Discharge from the suture site.

Apart from these complaints, they also suffer from psychological issues like feeling low mood, feeling neglected by others after the baby's birth and post-partum blues.

Me: **How do you reassure/treat them?**

Dr. Sathiya: One can never say a single generalized treatment for all complaints. With respect to the patient's specific complaints, the reassurance and treatment will vary accordingly.

–Look for signs of infection in the suture site such as redness, tenderness and discharge if the mother complaints of pain in suture site.

–Check for engorgement of breast and ask about the breastfeeding details, if the mother complaints of fever and pain in the breast.

–Ask a detailed history of number of pads per day, passage of clots if the mother complaints of heavy bleeding in the post-partum (Many a times, the mother wouldn't be actually having heavy bleeding at all). If there is post-partum hemorrhage, that mother has to be checked for retained placenta, etc. to find out the actual cause and treated accordingly.

–Counseling to family members about the need of care and attention to the new mom along with the baby in case if the new mom gives history of neglect by family members.

–Advice iron and calcium supplements for 6 months in post-partum for every new mom.

ME: **What are red flag signs in the post-partum that needs immediate expert care?**

Dr. Sathiya:

1. Abnormal/Excessive bleeding per vagina.
2. Fever.
3. Foul smelling discharge per vagina.
4. Discharge from suture site along with abnormal pin pricking pain which keeps increasing inseverity and redness in the suture site (episiotomy sutures in case of vaginal delivery and abdominal sutures in case of C-Section).
4. Breast engorgement with inability to feed the child.
5. Low mood.
6. Feeling arrogant towards her baby.

ME: **What are common myths about post-partum that you want to burst today?**

Dr. Sathiya:

MYTH 1: The mother should not take bath in early post-partum – No, she can. Infact, she has to take bath daily and she has to dry the suture site using a clean cloth after bath.

MYTH 2: The mother should drink only hot water –It is better to avoid ice cold water to avoid getting flu as her immunity would be low. She can still have normal water. There is no hard and fast rule that she should take only hot water.

MYTH 3: The baby should not be in an A.C. room – No. The baby can be in an A.C. room provided the baby is not comfortable or irritable, but ensure that the baby is always kept wrapped.

MYTH 4: The mother should only have vegetarian food in early post-partum – Not at all. The mother can have both vegetarian and non-vegetarian food. One thing to check on food is that it should be of less oil and less fried.

MYTH 5: A Big "NO" to sex in early few months of post-partum – It is a myth. Ideally, I advise the couple to refrain from sex for a period of 4–6 weeks in case of vaginal delivery and 6–7 weeks in case of C-Section, provided the suture site is healed well. If there is any pain, redness or discharge in the suture site, the couple has to wait till it heals completely.

MYTH 6: Using oral or IUD contraceptive like Copper-T can affect the baby's health. – Not at all. Both are safer methods of contraception and it is completely upto the couple to choose what they feel comfortable with.

ME: **What are the steps needed to be taken by a woman in pregnancy in order to prepare herself for post-partum?**

Dr. Sathiya: Actually, many women don't even think about post-partum during their pregnancy. Being a doctor, I myself wasn't much prepared about post-partum, all that I was thinking is that I'm going to have a baby.

What I tell to pregnant women who come for their antenatal visit is

–**To make a list of priorities** and should always give importance to those priorities than other things that come your way.

–**Prioritize rest** -For example, after child birth, there would be so many visitors coming day in and day out. If your baby is sleeping, be bold enough to say out to the visitors to excuse you so that you can nap for sometime.

–**Always have a helper for rescue** – How bold and an energetic person you may be, you still require a helper. It can be anyone like your mother, in laws, siblings, friends and your husband.

–**Set your expectation slow**-Never set high expectations about your childbirth, your baby and your post-partum of how it has to be. Every baby is different. Every mother is different. Never compare your post-partum journey with another woman which would make you start worrying.

–**Keep everything organized in prior** for your childbirth and post-partum. Keep your hospital bag ready which should include your dress, sanitary napkins, baby's dress, diapers, etc. Make everything ready and organized 1 month prior to your due date.

–**Nutrition is very important**. Concentrate on your diet. Never skip your meal. Eat healthy food.

–**Prepare yourself for post-partum**. I always say that post-partum period is not difficult. But it may be difficult if you are not prepared in prior.

ME: **What would be your advice to bring about a change in the existing health care to bring more awareness in pregnant woman regarding the post-partum?**

Dr. Sathiya: Many a times, the expectant mother has a lot of doubts which she would like to get clarified. Some expectant mothers even list down their queries in order to discuss with their doctor. But sadly, many doctors in both public and private healthcare are often too busy to sit down and talk with mother to get her doubts clarified. This scenario must be changed. The doctor must ensure to make time to talk with the expectant mother to discuss on her doubts, fear and worries.

Another important change is that the benefits of antenatal exercises and yoga have to be emphasized. Yoga plays a major role in both physical and emotional strengthening of the woman in antenatal and postnatal period. The irony is many yoga centers don't encourage antenatal women to participate due to the fear of developing complications in pregnant woman. But this is not true. This idea must be changed. Ideally, every area should have atleast one to two yoga centers for pregnant women. This would be of great help to an expectant mother.

Discuss the commonly anticipated events in the post-partum period (e.g., regarding breastfeeding, post-partum blues) to the expectant mother as well as her caretaker during the antenatal visit. One can also have printed pamphlets on the same in their clinic. Advise rest for a minimum period of 4 to 6 weeks and not to lift heavy weights.

Make the antenatal mother aware of red flag signs in post-partum period which should never be neglected and emphasize the need of immediate expert care.

ME: **What is the major difference between a first-time mother and a multiparous woman?**

Dr. Sathiya: First time mothers are **very anxious** when compared to that of multiparous (mother for more than one time) women. It is due to the fact that first time mothers have no prior experience and so they become very anxious about the baby's health. While coming to multiparous women, the **negligence towards self-care is higher** while compared to first time mothers. This is because they are already busy with the first kid and added to it, now they also have another kid which makes them super busy resulting in negligence of care towards self.

ME: **What would be your single golden advice for first time mothers, from a gynecologist perspective?**

Dr. Sathiya: Be prepared for your post-partum. Post-partum emotional wellbeing is very important. Keep it stable and steady by doing yoga, walking, exercises and maintaining a good rapport with your family. Motherhood is never a simple thing. Make sure you enjoy every bit of your motherhood journey by preparing yourself for your post-partum life.

INTERVIEW WITH THE PEDIATRICIAN

Contact Dr. Sudeendar (Pediatrician) through mail to meetsudeer@ hotmail.com.

Don't forget to use the CODE: OMGBABY10 to claim 10% discount on first online consultation with Dr. Sudeendar.

ME: **What are common complaints of a new mom related to her newborn health when she brings her child to a pediatric OPD?**

Dr. Sudeendar: First of all, nothing is simple for a new mom as she experiences it for the first time with her child. The commonest complaints would be regarding Vomiting, crying, peeing and pooping of the baby, certain physiological reflex/process in newborn like hiccups in the newborn, sneezing, sudden jerky movements, milk ejection from the nipples of baby, vaginal bleeding and discharge in female child, rashes in new born, milia (white spots in face during neonatal period) and physiological squint. Many of the above complaints are normal physiological processes and reflexes in a new born. To understand about these normal phenomena in baby, the new mom should always have an open conversation with the pediatrician (and never with the neighborhood).

ME: **What are common myths/wrong practices in child rearing?**

Dr. Sudeendar:

Common wrong practices are:

1. Applying sand over the milia: Milia is a normal physiological process in a newborn which will eventually decrease with time without any treatment.
2. Engorgement or milk ejection in new born is due to withdrawal of maternal hormones. Massaging the child's breast to reduce the engorgement in the breast will eventually worsen the entire problem.
3. In rural areas, people used to bathe the baby by making it lie on their legs with head down which leads to high chances of aspiration in baby. Always, the baby's head must be kept near the thighs and their legs near the feet while giving bath to avoid aspiration.

4. Giving gripe water or other native medicines: Mother's milk itself has all essential vitamins, minerals, water, immune booster and digestive enzymes. It has all that is needed for the newborn. No other medicines are required to aid the digestive process in babies.
5. Giving Donkey's milk – This should be completely avoided. It has a risk of posing threat to the newborn's health by causing diarrhea.

Me: **What is the major difference between a first-time mom and a second-time mom? How would you go about in reassuring them?**

Dr. Sudeendar: Mostly, first-time moms come with self-doubts. They don't doubt themselves unless everything is going well. But once the baby feels sick, the mother would start doubting herself about it. When it comes to second time moms, it is usually the feeling of guilt that they are not able to take care of the second child unlike the first child. For first time moms, I generally advise them that motherhood is a trial and error as they have no prior experience. So, they have to take things at ease without doubting themselves. For second or third-time moms, I always advise them to understand the first child's emotions and try to involve them to the maximum in taking care of the second child.

Me: **What is your recommendation for minimum age gap between first and the second child?**

Dr. Sudeendar: 4 years. By 4 years, the child will be able to understand that he/she is getting a new sibling and they will try to extend their best care towards the little one.

Me: **The most common worry of a new mom would be insufficient milk production. How could the mother have a check on whether she is producing sufficient milk for the baby?**

Dr. Sudeendar: There are four criteria to check if the mom is actually producing enough milk-

1. Average weight gain of 30 gms per day.
2. Child passing urine 6–8 times a day.

3. Baby sleeping for approximately 30 minutes continuously after feeding.
4. While feeding baby on one breast, Dripping of milk from the other breast.

Me: **Many new moms think that they are not producing enough milk if the size of their breast is small. Is it true?**

Dr. Sudeendar: No, the size of the breast is not related to the milk supply. It all depends on the ducts of the mammary glands.

Me: **Many new moms express and feed the baby with bottles. Is it advisable?**

Dr. Sudeendar: It is better to avoid bottles. Because once the baby is introduced to bottles, he/she may have nipple confusion. They may resist to latch onto mother's breast. It is ideal to feed the expressed milk through cup and spoon or paaladai (Antique milk feeding cup).

Me: **What are common lactation difficulties in new mom?**

Dr. Sudeendar: Sore nipples and inverted nipples.

Sore nipples: It is due to frequent washing of the breasts with soap and water, poor latching technique and pulling the baby away from the nipple while delatching. There are numerous medications available to treat sore nipples. Infact, breast milk itself is an excellent medication and it has to be applied over the sore nipple after each feed.

Inverted nipples: Breasts should be checked during the antenatal visits in order to avoid this confusion. Syringing is the most effective method to treat inverted nipples.

Me: **Whenever the baby cries, the family members would say that the baby is feeling hungry and would advise to feed the baby, irrespective of the time of last feed? What are the common causes of crying in a newborn?**

Dr. Sudeendar: Crying is the language of the newborn. They try to communicate their needs through crying. A baby will cry due to numerous reasons like wet diaper, feeing too cold or too hot, hunger, sleep and feeling insecure. If a mother feeds the baby for every crying, without knowing other methods of pacifying, there is a chance of overfeeding which could lead to diarrhea in the baby. New mom should not always try to feed her child because it is crying. Rule out other reasons for the child's cry. Try to pacify the baby by other means.

ME: **Another biggest concern or pain point of a brand-new mom would be developmental milestones in the baby. Many moms start stressing out if their child doesn't attain milestones on par with other known children of same age. What would you like to say to those mothers?**

Dr. Sudeendar: First of all, every baby is unique. Never compare your child with other children. Never discuss your child's milestones with other moms. Every milestone has a range. For E.g., people think that neck holding has to be attained by three months. But actually it takes three to six months.

ME: **Starting complimentary foods to the child is another biggest challenge to moms. When it comes to new moms, they would be having many doubts like what to start, when to start, how to start what to avoid, etc. Can you throw some light on the process of complimentary feeding?**

Dr. Sudeendar: A baby has to be exclusively breastfed for 6 complete months, after which he/she can be started with complimentary food. Always start with foods that are easily digestible like rice porridge. Avoid giving cow's milk and biscuits during the initial phase. It is advisable to start cow's milk once baby attains one year of age. Always check on the quality and quantity of the feed. Vegetables, fruits, nuts and grain can be introduced slowly one by one along the process. Give one new food at a time to check on allergic symptoms. When it comes to quantity, start with one spoon of prepared rice porridge flour and increase to three or four spoons depending on the baby's needs. Baby should be fed for minimum 4 times at 6–8 months of age. After 8 months, the feeds can be increased to 6 times a day.

ME: **What advice would you give for working moms on feeding the child during the exclusive breastfeeding days?**

Dr. Sudeendar: Ideally, if the mother has sufficient breast milk, I would suggest her to express the milk before leaving for work in the morning and store it in an airtight container which can be kept for 8 hours in room temperature and for 24 hours in a refrigerator. This can be fed to the baby by the caretaker at home. If the mother works in a place nearby to her home, I would advise her to come home during the lunch break to feed the baby on one breast and pump milk from the other breast which can be used to feed the baby in the afternoon.

ME: **What are red flag signs in baby that needs to be addressed immediately?**

Dr. Sudeendar:

- Irritable cry.
- Refusal of feed.
- Raise in temperature.
- Excessive vomiting.
- Color of the baby (pale/blue).
- Grunting.
- Lethargy.
- Withdrawal of chest during breathing.
- Seizures.
- Passing urine < 4 times a day (in newborn).

ME: **What is your single golden take away advice to new moms?**

Dr. Sudeendar:

Actually, I have 3 take away advice-

➢ Every vaccination visit for the child must be a discussion visit between the mother and the pediatrician regarding the following-

1. Anthropometry of the baby (growth).
2. Developmental milestones of the baby.
3. Feeding of the baby.

➢ Every baby is unique so never compare your baby's growth and development with the other babies.

- The mother's emotions are directly proportional to the production of breast milk. If you are happy, motivated and can bond with child well, you will be producing more milk. Whereas, if you are depressed and stressed out, you would be producing lesser quantity of milk.

INTERVIEW WITH THE PSYCHIATRIST

Contact Dr. Rajesh Kannan (Psychiatrist) through mail to psyrk2014@gmail.com. Don't forget to use the CODE: OMGMIND10 to claim 10% discount on first online consultation with Dr. Rajesh Kannan.

Me: **What are common symptoms of first-time moms when they are present in a psychiatrist Out Patient Department?**

Dr. Rajesh: First time moms don't usually come with a single clear-cut emotion, but with a variety of emotions ranging from fear, excitement and fulfillment to the extreme of crying, and inadequacy to be a mother. They say that they are afraid and in extreme cases, few say that everything that is happening around them don't seem real. It all feels like a dream. Everything around them had changed. They had changed a lot and don't seem like themselves anymore. In extreme cases, women would neglect their own child refusing to feed or go near the child. Few women would come up with obsession kind of complaints, mostly related to the safety of the child. They used to constantly check for the breathing of the child during nights. These are some of the emotions in post-partum blues and they are subjected to change with time and situation.

Me: **As per statistics, 1 in 9 women are affected by some form of depression. But is that the same number what you see in your practice? If it is underreported, what do you think are the most important causes that refrain women from talking out their problems openly?**

Dr. Rajesh: I definitely assume that the cases are underreported than the ground reality. Generally, most of the women assume that it is normal to be that way after childbirth. They feel that it is their fate/destiny to suffer through the new phase of life. Also, it is undetectable at initial stages unless physical problems like fever, swelling and pain can be seen where the people around the women can pick up the symptoms without even the women sharing about it.

Me: **What are three most common barriers to the new moms in accessing the expert help in mental health care?**

Dr. Rajesh:

1. Many women feel that it is normal to be that way. They think they are destined to go through such odd phase in life (similar to that of having cramps during menstruation).
2. Social stigma of branding her as insane and the family perception about her may change because of opening about her mental health issues.
3. They think that the treatment (medications/electro convulsive therapy) may affect the health and well-being of the child.

Me: **Though we all are now in an advanced world with modernized technologies, opening up about the mental health issues is still not accepted to be on par with physical health issues. How could we change this perception in people's mind?**

Dr. Rajesh: First, People need to accept that psychiatry is a part of medicine. It is purely based on science. It is not something about superstitious practice or magic. Like how the bones and joints are treated by an Orthopedician, brain or mind should be taken care by a neurologist or a psychiatrist. For example, if the brain is your hardware, the mind is your software. Brain related problems would be treated by a neurologist and the mind related problems would be treated by a psychiatrist. Everyone has to start seeing psychiatry as a part of science and they should realize that it is completely normal to have psychiatric problems like other physical conditions like diabetes, hypertension and that it is not a sin. One more thing is that, people around the person who is suffering from any form of psychiatric illness should come forward to help them seek treatment rather than absurdly advising them that the symptoms would fade away on its own in few days or months. If a person is suffering from a stroke, we cannot say that he will be fine in a few days even without any treatment. It is the same with psychiatric problems as well. One who is suffering needs to be motivated or helped to seek expert advice and start treatment at the earliest. It is always like "The Earlier, the better".

Also, it is always bi-directional – the person who is suffering has to speak out and the caretaker has to listen without any judgement and guide him/her to an expert for treatment.

Me: **Many-a-times the potential gap to assess the expert help in post-partum depression is huge such that it becomes severe when it reaches the psychiatrist for consultation, making a huge shift in treatment modality. How would you share your opinion on that?**

Dr. Rajesh: Yes, as you said, they are well ahead of mild and moderate symptoms when they seek the physician help. Any disease course will take its time to manifest in a severe form. If the woman is brought to treatment at an earlier stage, she may require a milder form of treatments such as counseling, Cognitive Behavioral Therapy rather than medications and Convulsive Therapy at a later stage. For example, I had seen a patient, a 23-year-old female, staff nurse by occupation who had delivered her first child four weeks earlier, presented with complaints of suicidal thoughts, thoughts of harming the baby and dissociative feeling. She said that nothing around her seems to be real. Everything is like a dream, everyone including her had changed. She doesn't look the same, even physically, like before. She had started feeling unrealistic, anxious, something-wrong-inside two weeks earlier and had opened out to her mother. She was reassured by her mother that it is normal to feel that way and had taken her to religious priests for some kind of native practices. But the symptoms haven't settled and started getting worse after which she was brought to the hospital. As she had suicidal and intrusive thoughts of harming the child, we couldn't wait for longer durations allowing medications to start acting in her body. We went ahead with electro-convulsive therapy (ECT) to reduce her symptoms. If the mother had awareness about the post-partum depression, she would have brought her daughter to a psychiatrist for consultation at a much earlier stage where she would have been treated with counseling sessions and medications.

Me: **Having said that, what are red flag signs of post-partum depression? How could one differentiate between post-partum blues and post-partum depression?**

Dr. Rajesh: Post-partum blues are generally a sign of transition phase where the woman starts adjusting and accommodating herself into the new phase of life with a little human being by her side, meeting the child's untold requirements all the time. Something similar to that of when you are moving to a new city where it takes some time for you to adjust to the new surroundings. It is because of the sudden decrease of hormones after child birth. It may usually last for two weeks starting from Day 3 or Day 4 of the post-partum. Most of the time the woman would be very sensitive and tearful. Post-partum blues are a mixture of emotions like excitement to being sad, fulfillment to worthlessness and responsible to self-doubting. It is subjected to change with time and situation. For example, one may feel so down and worthless but she could start feeling happy as she watches her favorite movie or just as the day progresses to evening.

But post-partum depression doesn't change over time or situation. They tend to remain sad, isolated and lack interest in anything and everything.

Red flag signs of post-partum depression would be-

1. Lack of sleep
2. Lack of appetite
3. Anhedonia –Lack of interest in everything
4. Neglect of self-care – doesn't like to bath or change clothes
5. Remains isolated, doesn't really want to involve in talking with others or discussions
6. Suicidal tendency
7. Intrusive thought of harming the child

These symptoms in any post-partum women should never be taken at ease. They should be immediately referred for psychiatric opinion and prompt initiation of treatment.

Me: **What is the major difference in mindset between a primiparous (first time mom) and a multiparous woman (mother for more than one time)?**

Dr. Rajesh: Majority of the anticipating first time moms are too young and unprepared for the child. In a country like India, till now majority of women are getting married in their late teens which make them anxious and are not really prepared to know what to expect when they are having a child. They have so many doubts and fear of responsibility of being a mom for the first time. When it comes to multiparous, they are already having the prior experience so they are aware of the process/post-partum changes and about the new born. The major difficulty of multiparous women would be managing the older children and the new born together. So post-partum depression is very common in first time moms when compared to women who are becoming mother for the second or third time.

Me: **Having a baby can lead to a gap between partners which can lead to relationship issues. What would be your advice for the couple on that?**

Dr. Rajesh: We also have something known as paternity blues in father where they envy the child for taking up their place in being close to their partner. One advice is that they have to prepare themselves to be a father to adjust with the new life. For example, when you become the manager of a company, obviously the post would come up with a set of new additional responsibilities. Similarly, when you take one step ahead from being a couple to becoming a family of three, you need to accept the new changes and responsibilities that come along with it. The couple has to allocate quality time for themselves – could be gardening, coffee time, cooking together or anything for that matter. Basically, they need to work out on a new schedule fitting their little one inside and still keep their relationship alive.

Me: **what are different treatment modalities for post-partum depression?**

Dr. Rajesh: For milder form, counselling or Cognitive Behavioral Therapy (CBT) would be helpful. For moderate, it would be combination of CBT and medications and also they need hospitalization. For severe form, one would require Electro Convulsive Therapy. There are newer advances where we use magnetic waves instead of ECT.

Me: **How about preparing the woman in the pregnancy phase to cope with their post-partum?**

Dr. Rajesh: As the saying goes, "Prevention is better than cure", it is a healthy practice that women need to be counseled about their post-partum during their pre-pregnancy or pregnancy phase. Many hospitals in metro cities have initiated the counseling sessions for pregnant women in helping them to mentally prepare for their new life as a mother. Even in government sectors, a lot of initiatives had been taken in recent years to reach out to the public at the primary health center levels. What we need is the horizontal collaboration of all specialists together as a team in providing a complete health care to the mom and the child (A Gynecologist, A Pediatrician and A Psychiatrist).

Me: **What is your single golden take away advice to new moms?**

Dr. Rajesh: Speak out your problems. Realize that asking for help doesn't make you a weaker soul.

INTERVIEW WITH FITNESS COACH

Contact Mrs. Kripa Dharmaraj (Fitness Coach) via www.kdvskg.com or through mail to kd@kdvskg.com. Don't forget to use the CODE: FITMOM20 to avail 20% discount on choosing any one of the programs under Kripa in www.kdvskg.com.

ME: **What are pain points of new moms when they approach you for weight loss?**

Kripa: The main pain point is losing their priority on process of newer responsibility of being a mother, taking care of the baby's needs, fulfilling family and society's expectation of being a responsible mother. When it comes to weight loss, priority is the top most important thing. Because how much diet/workout we suggest, until and unless they are going to prioritize themselves, it is never going to happen. Another important point is finding time. Baby gets their most of the time. Some babies follow a routine, while some don't. Some moms have a good support system, while some don't have. There are so many ifs and buts which could make their life little more challenging than the women who they used to be before the baby. So ideally, they need to be guided both physically and mentally to overcome the challenges rather than just telling them the kind of workouts and a strict diet plan.

ME: **Is the commercial fitness world complicating the process of weight loss?**

Kripa: I personally felt that it was too complicated which was one of the main reasons why I started this initiative back then. When I went to reduce 18 kgs, I did it much more easily with simple diet and habitual changes. No high intensity workout, no strict dieting, nothing. There is so much drama going on the fitness world, everything pointing to ultimately makeover money. Lot of them constantly promises "Quick weight loss" which is one of the most disturbing things to me because that might not be sustainable. So, when I had the privilege of seeing such amazing results with very simple methods, I am bound to go ahead and share it with people. Our body is just like a machine, like a car. We need to give the service required for the car in order to function well. Similarly, our body had gained weight over time so we need to give our body enough time to bounce back to normal in order to produce a sustainable effect.

ME: **As we were talking about the commercial fitness world, how do you and your KDvsKG differ from others? What is your USP-Unique Solution for the Problem?**

Kripa: Whatever may be the native food of their ethnicity, they could continue to eat their native food. I never advise any of my clients to eat specific food/vegetable/fruit just for the sake of weight loss. The main difference is that I don't give them menu plans. Three important problems with strict diet plans are – 1. They have to cook separately for themselves apart from what they prepare for the rest of the family, especially very difficult for a new mom with the child at home. 2. Everyone have certain native foods. Their body will accept that kind of food only. I am nobody to change that. 3. They get very bored when they follow the same kind of menu plan for the entire month. One of the main reasons why people don't stick on to the diet plan is BOREDOM.

One unique solution is that I give my clients what is called "THE MEAL FRAMEWORK" which would be personalized according to each and everyone of them. I teach them to be a "RESPONSIBLE EATER" putting them in the driver's seat. I always tell my community that if you learn swimming or cycling, you'll never forget it in your life time. Similarly, once they learn to eat responsibly, all that they need beyond is perseverance and consistency to keep following it. Another important strength is "COMMUNITY" – the gang feeling that makes them feel so much alive and feel that they are not alone.

Because even your family members may not empathize with you of what you go through, but when you are in a similar tribe, they can always understand you. It's a WhatsApp and a Facebook group, but the energy in the group is so lovely.

ME: **Getting an hour of continuous workout everyday can feel like a big challenge to new moms. Is there any way to break it up into multiple small sessions? What do you advise regarding the duration of workout?**

Kripa: I advise them to do 150 minutes of workout in a week. They can split it according to their convenience from as short as 10 mins to as long as an hour. It should include yoga, mobility and strengthening so that all muscles are involved in the workout. It should always be a level by level approach starting from cardio-to-stretches-to-mobility rather than jumping and hitting high intensity workout at the very beginning. Most important thing is, your body should be given enough nutrition before hitting intensive workout otherwise it could backfire instead of helping. Perseverance is the key to winning in all perspectives like nutrition and fitness but they definitely win. Keep small challenges/goals at the very beginning which could be achievable that way it is very motivating for the new moms. They should actually feel the success, which in turn brings the motivation to be consistent with their efforts. Motivation always happens after the first success.

ME: **That's great information. The new mom would be worried about the food because it should not cause more weight gain and at the same time shouldn't reduce their breast milk as well. If I am not stealing one of your nutrition modules, can you just give a rough outline of meal framework for the new moms?**

Kripa: Usually, the doctors would recommend an additional 200–500 extra calories other than the normal requirement. I cannot specifically give a particular framework in general to all new moms because as I said earlier the nutritional level would be different from person to person. One thing which I can advise them is to include fruits, vegetables, proteins and carbohydrates in a balanced way in their diet. Do not skip on carbohydrates thinking that it's the enemy. Carbohydrate is the main form of energy. You need energy to take care of yourselves and your baby.

ME: **Can you give a piece of advice on what foods to be avoided during the process of weight loss?**

Kripa: We cannot completely avoid anything thinking that it is a processed food. Right now, whatever we eat is processed. No one can completely avoid pizzas, pasta or noodles as our generation people are used to eating all these food over time. Our kids are even worse. One thing which we can concentrate is how to keep these food intake at a low frequency. We cannot completely eat "PROCESSED-FREE" food until and unless we grow everything by ourselves. It is impossible to be that way. I don't believe in "Restrictive Eating"because it can cause craving for more of it. My idea is to teach them to be in moderation. I always tell them to be practical about the food. Try to get into low processed foods. Keep it simple and native. Whatever food grows locally, say within the 80 km radius, eat that food. You need not eat kiwi or avocados or berries or oats just for the reason of weight loss. The simpler you keep it, the more you could actually follow it consistently over time.

ME: **What would be your single golden take away advice for new moms from the fitness perspective?**

Kripa: DON'T RUSH. You are beautiful the way you are. Take your own time to get things back on track. By the time the baby becomes like one or two years old, you will be back to shape. Baby will be little more independent and you would be more relaxed. Everything will fall in place eventually.

INTERVIEW WITH THE LACTATION CONSULTANT

Contact Mrs. Teena Abishek on www.pccindia.in or through mail to teenaimmanuel@gmail.com

Don't forget to use the CODE: **OMGPCCC10** to avail 10% discount on first online consultation with Teena Abishek in Pregnancy Care Center and

–Use the CODE: **OMGPCCP20** to get 20% discount on any one of online pre-pregnancy/pregnancy/lactation classes under Teena Abishek in Pregnancy Care Center.

ME: **What are common pain points of a new mom in lactation when they come for your consultation?**

Teena:

1. Identifying the hunger cues of the baby.

2. How to latch their baby for breastfeeding?

3. Self-doubting themselves for many things like whether they produce sufficient milk for the baby, whether they are feeding the baby properly etc.

ME: **How would you go about on managing/reassuring on these pain points?**

Teena:

One thing which I want to mention is that the phase of awareness about breastfeeding should never start after becoming a mom, rather it should start from the time when a woman is pregnant.

Reassurance is the hardest part. They are preoccupied with their thoughts and pieces of superadded advice from the community that their milk wouldn't be suffice and that she needs to start the baby on formula milk. Convincing the new mom is a great deal for the lactation counsellor. I need to make them understand that "Their breast is not a bucket; it is a river". After having hours of counseling, they'll start to have a little trust on their body as well as on the lactation counselor and start following their guidance.

When it comes to latching, each mother's journey is different. One important point to remember is "breastfeeding shouldn't hurt the mother". Hurting while breastfeeding can lead to discontinuation of breastfeeding and starting on formula feeds. This puts the mother on guilt that she is not able to feed her baby for a long time. They need to get the lactation counselor guidance at the earliest.

LATCHING TIPS AND TECHNIQUES FOR A NEW MOM:

–Stimulate the baby by rubbing the nipple around the mouth of the baby before initiation of breastfeeding. With this, the baby will open his/her mouth wide to latch onto the breast.

–The cheeks of the baby should not dimple on suckling.

-The mother will be able to see visible swallowing reflex. Along with that, she can hear the "click" sound on swallowing as well.

-The nipple should remain in round shape while de-latching. It shouldn't be pinched nipple or altered in shape. Pinched nipple indicates improper latching which will hurt the mother and on the long run, can cause sore nipples, bleeding and abrasions.

ME: **That is a great piece of information. As you were mentioning earlier about mother's doubts on whether she is feeding her baby adequately, how could a mother check about this?**

Teena: First of all, I would like to advice mothers not to download the growth charts from google. Nowadays, doctors do not check with growth charts, however mothers are so keen on checking the growth parameters of their child. It is not necessary to micromonitor the baby's weight. People think that chubby baby is the healthy baby as the marketing world had always pictured it that way in their ads. It's not like that. Usually breastfed babies would be thin and skinny.

There are some trackers for healthy weight gain in babies:

-The average weight gain in the baby would be around one kg per month in first six months. For example, if a baby weight was 3 kgs at birth, the baby should be around 6 kgs at three months of age and around 9 kgs at six months of age. Again, it is an average value, do not stick on to it. Due to hereditary or some other reasons, few babies may not gain much weight, in which case mother can rely on other markers.

-Urine output in the baby (average 6–8 times/day)

-Defecation in baby (average 2–3 times/day)

ME: **What are common breastfeeding myths you want to burst today?**

Teena:

MYTH 1: The breast milk production is solely dependent only on mother's diet – It is a myth. Food actually constitutes to a minor percentage in production of breast milk. In fact, 90% milk production depends on two hormones namely prolactin and oxytocin secreted by the pituitary gland in the brain.

MYTH 2: Drinking more water in mother can cause common cold in child – No, absolutely not.

MYTH 3: Breastfeeding will prevent getting pregnant –Well, breastfeeding has contraceptive effect but only about 20%, so another 80% you are at a risk of getting pregnant. One should always consult a gynecologist in choosing another mode of contraception to avoid pregnancy.

MYTH 4: When pregnant with second child, the mother should not breastfeed the first child – No, they can breastfeed the baby. Sometimes, the mother may feel tired due to morning sickness which may be a reason for not breastfeeding. But otherwise the mother can very well breastfeed the older children. Family support is very ideal to continue nursing.

MYTH 5: Copper-T is not a safe contraceptive – Copper-T is relatively a safe and a highly effective contraceptive.

ME: **As you were mentioning about the family support, you always recommend to enroll all your pre-pregnancy, pregnancy and post-partum classes as a couple. So, what is the partner's role in supporting the new mom?**

Teena: The journey should start before the arrival of the baby. What I meant to say is, they should take the responsibilities during the pregnancy session. I always insist "Don't say my wife is pregnant, try to say we are pregnant". When it comes to the family support, the family should know about breastfeeding. Due to prolactin surge in a new mom, she would be very fragile and may have so many doubts and feel puzzled. During this time, if her partner lends his hands of support, she will definitely go an extra mile in giving her baby the best. It is really the need of the hour to educate the partner on supporting the new moms.

ME: **During this COVID crisis, what are your pieces of advice to the breastfeeding moms to continue breastfeeding their babies?**

Teena:

That is a most frequently asked question in recent times. Every mother should follow personal hygiene like washing their hands before touching the baby. If a mother is COVID POSITIVE but healthy, she can still breastfeed the baby following strict personal hygiene measures like using mask, following hand hygiene and respiratory hygiene. If the mother is sick or has fear of transmitting the disease to the baby, then she can pump out the milk and feed the baby with the help of other healthy person in the family. If that is also not possible, then she could first give her body enough time to recover, to regain her strength without worrying about breastfeeding the baby. Later when she is fully recovered, she can still bring back her breastfeeding routine using re-lactation techniques, by stimulating prolactin and oxytocin hormones in her brain with the help of a lactation counselor. That's the power of those hormones.

ME: **That's a lot of information. Now coming to Teena's favorite topic "RE-LACTATION". I have never seen an interview of you without you mentioning about re-lactation. What is the reason behind it?**

Teena: The reason behind insistence of re-lactation is from my own story of breastfeeding my son. I breastfed my baby until six months of age. When he was six months old, I had a major surgery and was hospitalized for about four weeks. During the hospitalization, I couldn't breastfeed my baby because of which my milk supply went down and eventually dried up. Due to lack of awareness of re-lactation, I couldn't succeed in breastfeeding my baby thereafter. Being in medical field, I myself wasn't aware about this. Then I started thinking about what could be the awareness in a normal lay woman. That's why I always touch upon the re-lactation topic in all my interviews.

ME: **Can you tell in detail about what is re-lactation and how could a mother do it?**

Teena: Lactation is solely due to prolactin and oxytocin hormones secreted by pituitary gland in brain - what I call as *'hero hormones of breastfeeding'*. Stimulating these hormones can induce the production of milk thereby leading to breastfeeding. If the baby is young enough to readily latch on to mother's breast, it would be easier to have a successful re-lactation. If the baby had forgotten about how to latch, it would be little more challenging but still possible. The mother who is trying to re-lactate, must be patient, consistent and must follow all instructions given by the lactation counselor. During re-lactation, the hero hormones would be stimulated by certain technique which in turn would induce breast milk. Here, we don't give hormonal supplements. There is another process called "INDUCED LACTATION" for those women who are adopting a child, where she can still breastfeed that baby. If the woman had given birth earlier, she can re-lactate and breastfeed the adopted child just by stimulating the hero hormones in her brain. If the woman has never been a mother earlier, she can start taking hormonal therapy along with other techniques of re-lactation about 4 months prior to adoption so that she could actually breastfeed the child. A woman who couldn't experience the celebration of motherhood, can still experience this wonderful feeling of breastfeeding the child through this process of induced lactation.

ME: **What would be your single golden take home advice for new moms?**

Teena: Pregnancy is not a sickness. It is a celebration. Try to include your family members during this journey. When it comes to lactation, always trust your body that it can produce milk. As I said earlier, your breast is not a bucket to get empty, it is like a river so it will flow. If you need, take help from a lactation expert. Make the breastfeeding journey as a memorable one and not a pathetic one.

LIFE IS NEVER THE SAME, IT IS EVEN MORE BEAUTIFUL

NO MORE CHAOS:

No more sitting down sad when a challenge hits you hard. Instead you have a clear mind-map of the starting point (problem), action points (mental strategies) and the finishing point (your desired goal). This clarity is important to avoid any further chaos in mind which could threaten to hold back your desired life goals. Your black board is now carefully written/rewritten hiding all the old flaws. No more confusions! No more self-doubts! No more inferiority complex! And no more comparison to validate yourself!

If you consider the difficulties in every challenge that comes your way, it is going to take you nowhere. What will you be holding in your hands? Just nothing. It is you who are holding the stone very close to your eyes, closer to an extent that it completely blocks your vision as a result of which, you couldn't see anything in the world. Imagine the other way, if you are clear in thoughts, confident on yourself, not stressing out your inner peace for anything that comes your way, you are going to look into the opportunity in each challenge, which is going to take you anywhere and everywhere. What will you be holding in your hands now? Everything. Removing those self-doubts from your head and gaining back your confidence is like taking the stone few feet away from you so that you can actually realize how small the stone is.

LIFE IS MORE BEAUTIFUL:

Your journey of motherhood with so many mind-blocks within you is something similar to what appears as the locked and sealed infinity. You are obviously going round and round and reach nowhere. But removing these mind-blocks are like **unlocking the infinity** into a clean and neat line, which has a clear starting point (where you are now) and a clear ending point (where you want to be). I am sure you are going to reach your finishing line sooner and faster.

During the course of the book, if you ever thought, that these strategies are very simple which you have already known or surfed through internet, I want to tell you something important. YES, it is just these simple practical steps which you need to effectively implement in your life bringing about a great change in life. For instance, I would like to quote the book" The Miracle Morning" by Hal Elrod in which he puts forth the importance of waking early in the morning, spending time for our personal development. Hal speaks about the life S.A.V.E.R.S where he mentions the readers to follow certain habits like silence (meditation), affirmation, visualization, Exercise, Reading and Scribing. These are all something which we already knew, but putting it in an organized way and scheduling our time for practicing life S.A.V.E.R.S is what that makes these ordinary ideas extra-ordinary. Life is actually very simple. And every problem in this world has a simple solution which we missed/ kept undisclosed and started running when seeing the problems, instead of facing and chasing the problems in the first hand. Do not let others who barely even know you, validate your actions. Who are they to judge you? What qualifications do they possess to become the judge of your beautiful life? It must be you who should be the judge of your life, not anyone else. Acknowledge your capabilities, validate yourself and unleash your inner potential to lead that happy motherhood you have ever dreamt of. Life is so beautiful. After all it is your life, so live your life to the fullest.

UNLEASH THE 2.0 VERSION OF YOURSELF:

Once you have mastered your mind and got answers to your problems, start applying it into every situation possible. This would open a wide gate of opportunities and happiness in life, be it anything from parenting to personal development, work, home, relationship and career goals. I am sure your life is never going to be the same like before. It is going to be even more beautiful. The outlook at which you see a challenge is entirely different from how it was used to be in the past. I am not telling you that there would be no challenges in your life. But after this book, if you start applying the mental strategies what we have discussed so far, there will be definitely a huge change in your attitude towards the challenge. It would be somewhere from "WHY ME?" to "TRY ME!" kind of attitude.

You are now fresh, rejuvenated, relaxed and ready to face everything with your own way of handling things. You are very clear that you need not fit into anyone's clauses and terms. You make your own rules. You are unique. You are special and you are the best mom your child could ever have.

I have taken a survey with many new moms to analyze their problems and their unique solution and one thing which they had in common is they were all self-doubting their abilities which was a stumble block in their early motherhood. Over months or years, they have realized that it is their own mind-block holding them from pushing towards their goal. They have learnt to roll that rock of mind-block to a side, so that they can travel comfortably and happily through their motherhood journey. But this had taken months or years to understand what that missing element was in their life as a mother and to take action. By that time, they realized that they had missed enjoying those beautiful quality moments with their little one. I don't want you to commit the same mistake and go through the same pain as those mothers, including me. That is the sole purpose of this book.

CONCLUSION

Thank you so much for being patient and read till the end of my book. I appreciate yourself-motivation to take charge of your life, to mold yourself into a happy, confident and composed woman who can now balance all the balls of your juggling game at a controlled pace. You have now learnt to trust your abilities, to have faith on yourself, to foresee the upcoming challenges and to be always prepared to face them with a positive and motivated mindset. You have now realized that the real change in attaining your desired lifestyle must begin within you. You will now have your feet grounded to fight all the challenges. So, don't wait, just go ahead and implement it in your life to see the much awaited positive outcomes. If you find this book useful, then please do me a favor by gifting this book to your friends, relatives, colleagues, family members and whomever you think would benefit from this book. If possible, get them a new copy of the book and give them as a gift to cherish. Let us together bring about the change in millions of new moms' life. Let us support each other without any judgement and grow together to achieve our goals in our lives.

CONNECT WITH THE AUTHOR

Feel free to drop me your message, reviews and personal experience after implementing the action points in your life to **vabinayambbs@gmail.com**. I am open to all honest feedbacks. Checkout my website **www.drabinayavijayakumar.com** to watch the expert interview videos using the link in the free bonus section.

ASK FOR REVIEW

If you really liked and enjoyed reading my book, I request you to write a review for my book on amazon.com website. Your review can help many brand-new moms to get this book and experience the maximum benefit out of the book.

RECOMMENDED BOOKS TO READ

10 MINUTE DECLUTTER by S.J. Scott

SIMPLY CLEAN BY by Becky Rapinchuk

Non Verbal Communication by Marshall R. Rosenberg

The Fifth Trimester by Lauren Smith Brodey

Infinite walk - by Deborah Sunbeck

Job Escape Plan by Jyotsna Ramachandran

4-Hour Work Week by Tim Ferriss

ACKNOWLEDGEMENT

To my mother: Amma, thank you so much for everything you have done to me in my life so far. Being a single mom, you have been a warrior to give the best to both of us. I have always admired you for your courage. I have taken you as my role model in being a mom. It is only because of you and your sacrifices, I am here today.

To my brother: Though we fight like Tom and Jerry, nothing can replace you in my life. We share a unique bond of love and affection that words can hardly express. Thank you Santhu.

To my husband: Pragee, You have been an immense pillar of strength to me ever since we met. You are not just my husband, but my best friend and a second father. You are a pure blessing in my life. Thank you for supporting me always.

To my in-laws: You have been my constants and selflessly encouraged me in every new attempt in my life. Gowri ma, without you I would have never even thought of writing a book, having an infant at home. You are a gem of a person I have ever met in my life.

To my author coach, Jyotsna Ramachandran: Before approaching you, I just had this rough message in mind, but had no idea of how to deliver it to the world. You have showed me that "A pen is mightier than a sword". Thank you so much for constantly guiding and mentoring me in this authoring journey.

To Author Success Academy members: Thank you for helping me selflessly with all your suggestions and feedbacks every time when I had any confusion in the process of authoring this book.

To experts who agreed to give interview for this book: Thank you Dr. Sathiya, Dr. Sudeendar, Dr. Rajesh Kannan, Mrs. Kripa Dharmaraj, Mrs. Teena Abishek for adding more value to my book.

www.ingramcontent.com/pod-product-compliance
Lightning Source LLC
Chambersburg PA
CBHW062111160726
48282CB00026B/755
* 9 7 8 8 1 9 4 8 0 5 8 2 3 *